Praise for
Teresa James: WAFS PILOT . . .

Teresa James lived in an era when women had little control over their lives. At 19, she learned to fly when aviation was still a wondrous and dangerous venture. She had the grit, guts, and tenacity to develop exceptional flying skills and became a professional "barnstorming" stunt pilot.

When the United States entered World War II, Teresa volunteered to fly military aircraft. She and 27 other members of the Women's Auxiliary Ferrying Squadron (WAFS) stepped into newly created roles—daring, dangerous jobs flying newly designed, newly built airplanes in incredibly challenging conditions.

In this fast-paced, engaging book, author Sarah Byrn Rickman captures the story of an irrepressible woman who flew her way into the history books. This book is a gift to aviation buffs, to World War II historians and, most of all, to young girls and boys who will be inspired to step up, take risks, and tenaciously pursue their own dreams.

–SUSAN WITTIG ALBERT, author of *The General's Women*

Sarah's wonderful book brings to mind what an incredible life force Teresa James was. Her story and her vitality still serve as an inspiration to today's young women. From a personal standpoint, the impression Teresa left on me and my daughters is grand, and I still miss her to this day. I consider it a privilege to have known her and to call Teresa "friend"—because to know her was to love her.

–JULIA LAURIA-BLUM, Creator of the WASP exhibit, American Airpower Museum, Farmingdale, New York

Teresa James was a bold and gutsy pilot, with a wicked sense of humor. This book does her huge personality justice. Sarah does it again with a spot-on account of the life of an original WWII ferry pilot.

–JACQUELINE BOYD, PhD., Chair, Amelia Earhart Memorial Scholarship Fund, The Ninety-Nines, Inc.

Sarah is so good at getting into the soul of her characters, and this book is no different. I was transported right into the cockpit as Teresa James was flying one of her missions. Sarah's work is always inspiring and enjoyable to read!

—COMMANDER CLAUDIA MCKNIGHT, U.S. Coast Guard pilot (Ret.)

A young adult story of a barnstorming pilot turned WWII ferry pilot, this is a worthy companion to Sarah's previous works. It portrays the challenges faced by a young woman in the 1930s, learning not only to fly, but to master aerobatics.

—CAPT. LUCY YOUNG, U.S. Navy pilot (Ret.); airline pilot retired

Sarah brings to life the story of Teresa James, a most determined young woman. Exceptional flying skills, combined with female pluck and persistence, put her in the cockpit flying for the USA in World War II.

—MARY TRIMBLE, author of *Tenderfoot*—a novel based on a first-hand adventure of the eruption of Mount St. Helens

Yet again, Sarah brings to life the personality and sense of adventure of one of the first women to fly for the U.S. military.

—ERIN MILLER, Author of *Final Flight, Final Fight*, chronicling the fight to have her WASP grandmother buried at Arlington National Cemetery

Teresa James
WAFS PILOT

**Gear Up/Gear Down
✢ A P-47 to Newark ✢**

Teresa James waves from Ten Grand's cockpit as she prepares to take off for the docks at Newark, New Jersey, September 1944. Ten Grand was the 10,000th P-47 Thunderbolt built by Republic Aviation during World War II. *From the author's collection with personalized message from Teresa, March 2000*

Teresa James
WAFS PILOT
Gear Up/Gear Down
✈ A P-47 to Newark ✈

by Sarah Byrn Rickman

FLIGHT TO DESTINY PRESS
Colorado Springs, CO

ISBN: 978-1-7350595-1-8
Library of Congress Control Number: 2021913959
Copyright © 2021 Sarah Byrn Rickman. All Rights Reserved.

Published by Flight to Destiny Press, Colorado Springs, CO 80907

No part of this book may be mechanically or electronically reproduced without written permission of the publisher. For information, contact Flight to Destiny Press at 937-581-0837 or sarahbyrnrickman@gmail.com.

Cover Image Courtesy: *Thanks to both the WASP Archives, Texas Woman's University Library, Denton, and the International Women's Air & Space Museum, Cleveland, Ohio, for copies of this great photo.*
Cover & Interior design by Robert Schram, Bookends Design

Manufactured in the United States of America

Cover caption: Teresa James, the eighth woman pilot to qualify for the WAFS (Women's Auxiliary Ferrying Squadron) in World War II, is ready to fly any aircraft the U.S. Army Air Forces throws at her.

Dedication

THIS BOOK IS DEDICATED to six women pilots from World War II who introduced me to the WAFS—the Women's Auxiliary Ferrying Squadron—described their wartime flying experiences, and then told me their stories.

The third week in June 1999, on the invitation of my WAFS friend and mentor-to-be, Nancy Batson Crews, I met and personally interviewed five of her fellow original WAFS: Gertrude Meserve Tubbs LeValley, Barbara "BJ" Erickson London, Barbara Poole Shoemaker, Florene Miller Watson, and Teresa James Martin.

Teresa James, WAFS Pilot is the third biography to come out of that, for me, extraordinarily historic meeting. It follows *BJ Erickson: WASP Pilot* (2018) and *Nancy Batson Crews: Alabama's First Lady of Flight* (2009).

Sarah Byrn Rickman, June 2021

Contents

One: Me, a Barnstormer? — 1

Two: Giuseppe Faranessi's Pants — 9

Three: Dink and Teresa Say "I Do" — 15

Four: New Castle Army Air Base — 19

Five: The Originals — 25

Six: The First Ferrying Flight — 33

Seven: Destination: Great Falls, Montana — 39

Eight: Six Yellow Stearman PT-17s — 47

Nine: Twenty-eight Women Qualify as WAFS — 57

Ten: Teresa Takes Hollywood by Storm — 65

Eleven: Yes, the WAFS Will Fly Fighter Aircraft — 69

Twelve: Seven WAFS Calgary Canada Bound — 75

Thirteen: "Ever Flown a P-51?" — 83

Fourteen: Teresa Returns to NCAAB, Dink Heads Overseas — 91

Fifteen: Bad News — 97

Sixteen: Ten Grand — 103

Seventeen: The Last Supper — 109

Eighteen: Dink—D-Day Plus Forty Years — 119

Epilogue — 123

Postscript — 127

Appendix 1: Teresa James' Brief Biography	129
Appendix 2: Some of the Aircraft Teresa James Flew during WWII	131
Appendix 3: Teresa James' Aviation Timeline	135
Appendix 4: Glossary and Acronyms of WWII Aviation and Military Terms Used	139
Appendix 5: General Glossary	143
Appendix 6: Bibliography	145
Acknowledgments	149
About the Author	151
Other Books by Sarah Byrn Rickman	153
A Note from Sarah	155
Sarah's Book Awards	157

Air Transport Command wings worn by the 28 Original WAFS. *Courtesy Joe Weingarten*

An A-25 Curtiss dive bomber with the Army Air Forces star on the left wing and the fuselage. *Courtesy: National Museum of the United States Air Force*

Chapter One

Me, a Barnstormer?

October 1944

I picked up a sick A-25 dive bomber out West and nursed that baby all the way to the East Coast. It took several days to make the trip. First, I couldn't get the gear up, so I had to stop and have that fixed. Then the radios went out, and I stopped at another base. Next, I couldn't get the bomb-bay doors closed.

On the final leg of the flight, as I was approaching Aberdeen, Maryland—my destination—exhaust fumes poured into the cockpit, and I had to request a straight-in approach. They cleared me. I had to land with the cockpit canopy open and the wind blowing in my face. It was hard to see my exact height above the ground.

As the wheels touched the runway, the control tower operator said, "That was a beautiful landing."

"You ought to see me grease 'em in when I'm not applying my lipstick," I replied.

I walked into Operations to get my Memorandum Receipt signed for the aircraft and told them how much trouble I had getting there in one piece.

The officer said, "Well, no wonder. It's a Class 26 airplane."

"What does that mean?" I ask.

Teresa and the OX-5 Travel Air, the aircraft she flew first and in which she earned her license in 1934. *Courtesy: International Women's Air & Space Museum, Cleveland*

"They'll taxi it out to the Aberdeen Proving Ground and use it for bombing practice," he explained. "The pilots will bomb the hell out of it to find out how accurate their air strikes are."

[That was when Teresa James learned that some of the airplanes she and her fellow women pilots were ferrying were headed for the boneyard. In other words, they were being scrapped.]

After that, flying junk airplanes gave me more than a few gray hairs.

+ + +

March 2, 2000, Lake Worth, Florida

"How are ya, honey?" the gravelly voice greets me through the screen. "Come on in, the coffee pot's on."

Teresa James and I sit at her dining room table and stir our coffee. Framed black-and-white photographs of Teresa—vintage 1930s and '40s—cover one wall.

There's Teresa, twenty years old—clad in jodhpurs, a zip-front leather vest over a long-sleeved blouse, and a leather flying helmet—standing beside a Travel Air OX-5 biplane. She has the same devil-may-care look as the woman sitting across from me. Only now the face is lined with character and age.

The unruly black curls evident in all the vintage photos have given way to unruly blonde ones. "They said blondes have more fun. I decided to find out for myself." The merry brown eyes miss nothing, and the smile that won friends, male and female, from Long Island to Long Beach, from Alaska to West Palm Beach—and Hollywood—lights up the already warm south-Florida day.

Teresa launches into a tale of how in 1933, at age nineteen, she learned to fly.

"It was a man, of course"—and laughs.

"I was never interested in flyin', but my brother Francis was. He and two of his friends took off one Sunday from this field outside of Pittsburgh—it wasn't an airport, just a field surrounded by trees and wires. They were going to Detroit but only got as far as Cleveland. They ran into high winds, ran out of gas, and crash landed. My brother's leg was broken, bad.

"When he got out of the hospital and was home, he couldn't drive, so he got me to drive him to the airport. I told him he was crazy, but I took him. He got me out there listening to these guys hangar flyin'.

"On Sunday, these guys' girlfriends would pack picnic baskets and they'd all fly off somewhere and have a picnic. They tried to get me to go along, but I wasn't havin' anything to do with flying.

"Then, one day, this beautiful silver airplane lands and out steps this Greek god. Oh wow! I want to meet this guy bad.

"He says to me, 'where you been hidin'?' Then he asks me to go flying with him the next weekend.

"I said no, and then I coulda killed myself. Already, I was really nuts about that guy. His name was Bill."

Two weeks later, Teresa did go flying with Bill.

"I sat stiff as a board in that airplane, my feet tucked down by those rudders.

"It was a trainer airplane with an open cockpit, tandem—one seat behind the other—and I sat in front. I had a full set of controls in front of me, just like he had in front of him. I was scared to death that I'd move and accidentally touch one and throw the airplane into a spin, and we'd both be killed."

Terrified, Teresa sat with her ankles frozen in one position. "When I got out of the plane at the picnic spot, I could hardly walk.

"Oh, I had a good time while I was there, but all I could think about was when I had to climb back in the airplane again. God, I was petrified."

Then Teresa learned that Bill had gone to Chicago to take an airline job. Still, she continued to drive Francis to the Wilkinsburg Airport. She refused any further offers of airplane rides until Harry Fogle flew into her life.

"Harry was fresh out of Parks Air College in St. Louis, Missouri. Francis kept needling me. 'Why not learn to fly and surprise Bill when he comes back,' he says. 'Get Harry to teach you. I dare you.'"

Teresa was never one to turn down a dare. A week later, Harry Fogle sat in the front seat of the 1920s vintage OX-5 Travel Air biplane waiting for her to climb in behind him.

Teresa, standing on the lower wing, took a deep breath, swallowed her terror, and pulled a leather helmet over her protesting curls. She threw her right leg over the side of the open cockpit and stepped down on the seat. When she was seated, both feet resting on the rudder bar, she tugged her goggles over the helmet and secured them. She reached for the lap belt, pulled it across her stomach, fastened it, and pulled it very tight.

Sitting in that open-to-the-air cockpit on a lovely July morning, she was as ready as she'd ever be for her first lesson.

Once in the air, Harry put the airplane in a shallow turn to the left, dipping the left wing down. Teresa looked over the side of the plane and quickly shut her eyes.

"Oh, my God! I was so scared. I reached forward and tapped him on the shoulder. When he turned around, I mouthed 'please . . .' and motioned at the ground below.

"Through the gosport tube [a voice tube through which flight instructors give instructions to a student] he said, 'Put your feet on the rudders and your right hand on the stick. Keep 'em there. Feel what I'm doing.'

"All I felt was the wind on my face and that sinking feeling in the pit of my stomach."

Gradually Teresa began to follow Harry's movements. She thought she was simply moving the control stick and the rudders in concert with him. Back on the ground, she learned that she actually was flying the airplane. Harry had taken his feet and hands completely off the controls.

"That airplane had no airspeed indicator. The singing of the wind in the wires and your own ears tell you how fast you're going." [Biplanes have two wings. The wings are held together by several crisscrossed wires. The wires vibrate in the wind and "sing".]

The instrument panel offered Teresa little help—an oil gauge, temperature gauge, and an altimeter, which measures altitude. The fuel gauge, a wire on a cork bobber, was located outside the windscreen [window] on the engine cowling [cover].

"The Travel Air had no brakes—I found that out when he had me land it. No tail wheel, just a tail skid, which was fine because we were landing on grass. You had to learn how to taxi it, keeping the skid up and off the grass."

Teresa took a couple more lessons. Two weeks later, Harry called her early.

"He said it was a good morning to fly, so come on out. I had a total of four hours and twenty minutes in the air. After two practice landings, Harry got out of the airplane, picked up the tail, turned the plane around, and told me to take it up—solo!"

Without Harry's weight, the biplane literally jumped into the air as Teresa ran it along the grass.

"By the first turn at Grand Boulevard, I was two hundred feet too high. By the second turn, over the house that was our landmark, I was four hundred feet too high. My legs were shakin' on the rudder bar, and I'm prayin' I'll get back on the ground safe.

"When the wheels finally hit the grass, I tried to remember how Harry stopped the thing. All I could remember was taxiing for a long time and then the tail skid settling into the grass, and the airplane just kinda stoppin' of its own accord.

"So that's what I did. I let it roll. I was shaking so bad, I swore I'd never get back in an airplane again. But, of course, I did."

A few weeks later, a flying circus came to town. "There was this stunt pilot who was trying to date me. He kept tellin' me he wanted to get me up in an airplane and teach me all these maneuvers.

"'Teresa,' he said, 'we can make a stunt pilot out of you, and you can make a lot of money.'

"I liked the sound of that. And there was Francis, again, telling me how Bill would be so proud of me, learning how to fly. If I could do all these fancy maneuvers, he'd be even more impressed.

"So I went up with this stunt flyer.

"We did a wing over. There I was hanging by my seatbelt in mid-air. The sky had disappeared, and there was nothing but air between me and the ground. Stomach, I thought, stay with me now or somebody down below will get rained on.

"Then we did a hammerhead stall, with the plane fallin' back on its tail, and then a loop. Once again, I wanted to grab for the sissy bars on the side of the cockpit. But then he had me try it. I took the controls and began to get the hang of it. I was on my way to becoming a stunt pilot. I started adding up all that money I was gonna make, and we hadn't even landed."

+ + +

And the eighty-six-year-old sitting across from me who, but for the gravel in her voice, talks like she's still nineteen, pauses. She fixed me with those sprightly eyes of hers and laughed.

"Not long after that, we got word that Bill had gone and got married. I was devastated. He had no idea I had this crush on him. Breaks o' the game."

But by then, Teresa was doing stunts with Harry Fogle. "Teresa James, Girl Stunt Pilot and Harry Fogle, The Flying Iceman," the flyer read. Teresa and Harry became a regular double feature in airshows around Pennsylvania.

"I made my debut with 12½ spins then went home and showed my mother how much money I made. Fifty dollars! She said, 'Stay with it!' She really encouraged me!" That was a lot of money in the 1930s!

Teresa kept working on those spins, building up to more of them. Eventually, she thrilled airshow audiences with 26½ tail spins followed by a series of loops in the OX-5. That sequence required that she fall from an altitude of 9,800 feet to 1,200 feet above the ground before coming out of those dizzying spins.

This thrilled audiences because the airplane appears out of control, yet the pilot does have control of the aircraft.

Though she had worked hard to acquire that kind of nerve and skill, Teresa still claimed that even when she had more than fifty hours in the air, she still was scared. "That helped me later on when I began instructing, 'cause I could relate to how the student felt, how scared he might be. I could always tell by their body language. I'd been there."

Teresa received Private License #31249 on October 12, 1934. She was twenty years old. The world of flight was waiting for her on an 80-horsepower, single-engine platter. World War II and the Women's Auxiliary Ferrying Squadron (WAFS), and the events that would change her life were still eight years away.

Chapter Two

Giuseppe Faranessi's Pants

TERESA AND I HAVE BEEN TALKING for more than an hour. The tape recorder is whirring away.

In front of us are scrapbooks full of photos. In one, she's wearing a mid-calf white dress, high heels, elbow-length gloves, and a wide-brimmed, white "picture hat" worn at a jaunty angle. Another shows her holding a bouquet of gladiolas in one hand and a mail sack in the other.

That's when she was chosen by her hometown, Wilkinsburg, Pennsylvania, to fly the mail as part of National Mail Week, May 15-21, 1938, celebrating the twentieth anniversary of American Air Mail delivery.

In contrast, another photo shows her decked out in a bulky winter flying suit.

What the photos have in common, other than her image, is that there is always an airplane in the photo—and an occasional good-looking man.

Teresa James is not only exceptionally attractive, her brown eyes always seem to laugh, and her wide smile just barely hides the hint of the wise crack about to escape her lips. She is known for both her wicked sense of humor and her unruly and abundant black curls.

Daredevil only begins to describe her. Using her incredible stamina, she trained herself to be a marathon dancer and won sev-

Wilkinsburg, Pennsylvania's hometown girl pilot, Teresa James, is ready to fly the mail, May 1938. *Courtesy: International Women's Air & Space Museum, Cleveland*

eral contests. She took up ice skating and turned out to be a natural, cutting a fine figure on the ice. She did, however, have one skating mishap. The local newspaper picked up the story. *Laughs At Sky Perils, Gets Cut Skating* read the headline.

Teresa told the reporter, "I get my thrills in the air. I've never had a scratch flying."

Flying was now her life. She flew a blue airplane and wore a white helmet. She was best known for those 26½ turns in the air, finally pulling out of the spins at 1,200 feet above the ground. Early in her flying career she made two forced, but successful, landings due to engine trouble. "Any landing you walk away from is a good landing." In her spare time Teresa flew airplanes for parachute jumpers.

✈ ✈ ✈

I was in for an even better story.

"Did I tell ya about the time I popped the buttons off Giuseppe Faranessi's pants?" Teresa asks, turning to the page with the photocopy of her advanced instructor's license.

"No," I answer. "Who was Giuseppe Faranessi?"

"I had already gotten my Primary Instructor's Rating from Buffalo Aeronautical in New York, in August 1939. Now I was ready for my Secondary. By the winter of 1940-'41, I had saved enough money to go for a course in Advanced Aerobatic and Inverted Flying. [Inverted means flying upside down. Aerobatics are daredevil stunts performed by an airplane in flight.]

"That's what I needed to teach in the Army Cadet program. There were rumors of the U.S. maybe getting into World War II. I would be teaching young men looking at flying combat.

"I was told that Max Rappaport's Flying Service at Roosevelt Field on Long Island had the best flight instructors for aerobatics, so that's where I went. Bill Pyhota was my instructor.

"First I had to convince him that his efforts to scramble my brains in the air weren't going to send me packing. When we came to the understanding that I was sticking, we got down to business.

"Finally, the day came for my flight test. I waited in the pilot's lounge and listened to three male pilots waiting for their tests. They were discussing how tough the Civil Aeronautics Administration (CAA) Flight Examiner, Giuseppe Faranessi, was. I was number four scheduled to fly—after all of them.

"Faranessi's reputation was confirmed real fast! He flunked two of the guys before I got to fly. Then I overheard Bill telling him there was a mechanical problem with the plane I had been flying.

"His reply was, 'Let her fly the new one you got this morning. If she can fly one, she should be able to fly 'em all.'

"I started for the plane and got in the front seat—like I always did. He said, 'Get in the back, I'll fly the front seat.'

"I'd never flown that plane from the back seat. The attitude [orientation of the aircraft in relation to the horizon] appears different from the back. But I climbed into the back seat.

"When we get up, in this commanding voice he continues telling me what to do. First order, 'A slow roll to the left.'

"I did it. Right on the money.

"Then he did a couple. I didn't think they were any great shakes.

"'Your trouble is, you're not exerting enough pressure on the stick,' he tells me.

"OK buster, I thought, this one you'll remember. I popped the control stick so fast he was straining against the seatbelt. Then in a very calm voice he asked me to do a two-and-a-half-turn spin to the right.

"I was so intent on doing my best, I didn't realize I was frantically chewing my gum. It's such a good tension reliever. Then I caught him looking in the rearview mirror, his jaw pumpin', mocking me chewing my gum.

"When we got down, Faranessi didn't say a word."

He walked away, leaving Teresa standing by the plane unbuckling her parachute harness.

"Bill asked how I did.

"I said, 'I don't know. He didn't tell me.'

"Then Max, the boss, appeared. He motioned me to come in the office.

"There stood Giuseppe Faranessi holding up his pants with one hand and his suspenders with the other.

"'Young lady,' he said, 'Any woman who can pop the buttons off my pants at 7,000 feet deserves a ticket. You damn near catapulted me outta the plane!'

"I had passed!"

Teresa, having earned her Secondary rating, was now qualified to teach combat aerobatics to young men who wanted to fly fighters in the coming war. She went home and landed a job at Pittsburgh's Tomak Aviation Corporation as a flight instructor.

Newlyweds, Mr. and Mrs. George Martin. *Author's personal collection*

Chapter Three

Dink and Teresa Say "I Do"

TERESA HAD BEEN DATING one of her former flight students, George "Dink" Martin. Hoping to marry her, Dink had popped "the question" a couple of times, but she was totally engrossed in teaching America's future fighter pilots the maneuvers that would keep them alive if the U.S. entered the war in Europe. She said "no."

Then came December 7, 1941. That Sunday morning, Japanese warplanes caught the United States, its military, and its people off guard with a bombing attack. Japanese aircraft sank most of the U.S. Navy fleet anchored at Pearl Harbor, Honolulu, Hawaii.

The following day, President Franklin D. Roosevelt announced that Congress had voted to declare war on Japan and its ally, Nazi Germany. World War II had come to the United States, and able-bodied men flocked to the Army enlistment sites. Dink Martin was one of the many.

By spring 1942, Dink, was stationed with the 6th Photographic Squadron at Peterson Field in Colorado Springs, Colorado. Teresa put in for vacation time at her job at Tomak in Pittsburgh, and she, her sister Betty, and Dink's mother drove west to visit him. Once again, Dink pressed her to marry him.

Teresa had dreamed of a big wedding, but circumstances had changed. She said "yes."

Teresa's name was well known in the aviation celebrity world—thanks to her barnstorming fame—but she and Dink wanted to keep the news of their marriage out of the press. They made their plans and told no one. Teresa didn't even call her mother. They planned to do that later.

Mrs. Martin (Dink's mother) and Betty, Teresa's Maid of Honor, were the only family in attendance. The bride and her attendant wore their Civil Air Patrol uniforms for the ceremony. Teresa and Dink said their vows in secret.

In spite of their efforts, the next day a newspaper carried the story: "Famous Stunt Pilot Married." Teresa's days on the barnstorming circuit and her famed twenty-six tailspins followed by a series of loops in the OX-5 had caught up with her.

"My mother picked up the paper back in Pittsburgh and damn near had a heart attack. She was hurt about it," Teresa wrote. Dink's mother and Betty went back to Pittsburgh and Teresa remained in Colorado Springs with Dink.

Two weeks after the wedding, Dink Martin was assigned to flight school and immediately transferred to Santa Maria, California, for primary flight training. Wives were not welcome at the training base, so Teresa went back to Pittsburgh to teach at Tomak Aviation.

✥ ✥ ✥

Early in World War II, the United States did not have enough qualified male pilots to fight the war that had been thrust upon us on December 7, 1941.

Totally unprepared, the United States was plunged into a major two-front war. In the Pacific, the country was pitted against the Empire of Japan. Across the Atlantic, in Europe, we went to war with Japan's ally, Nazi Germany.

Men who were qualified pilots and not already in the military—men like Dink Martin—joined up immediately. The United States needed to train more pilots as quickly as possible. But a few months

Nancy Love, founder and leader of the original WAFS and later—after Jacqueline Cochran was named Director of Women Pilots—leader of the WASP who ferried aircraft for the Ferrying Division, Air Transport Command, U.S. Army Air Forces. *Courtesy: WASP Archive, Texas Woman's University Library, Denton*

into the war, the planes that had been built to train those new pilots sat idle at the factories. There were not enough qualified male pilots available to fly those new planes to the flight training schools.

Why not try using experienced women pilots to ferry (fly) those aircraft to the flight schools?

Nancy Harkness Love, a well-known and well-respected 28-year-old woman pilot, sold Colonel William H. Tunner, commander of the

Ferrying Division, Air Transport Command, U.S. Army Air Forces, on the idea of using women pilots to deliver those trainer aircraft from the factories to the flight schools. Colonel Tunner hired Nancy to find qualified women pilots and to organize and lead what became the Women's Auxiliary Ferrying Squadron (WAFS) of World War II.

On September 5, 1942, Air Transport Command (ATC) commanding officer General Harold L. George, Colonel Tunner's boss, received the OK from U.S. Army Air Forces Headquarters that he had been waiting for. Nancy Love could begin recruiting women pilots. Telegrams went out to eighty-three women Nancy thought could qualify to fly Army training aircraft from factories to flight training schools around the nation.

On September 6, 1942, Teresa was working as a flight instructor at Tomak when, just like some eighty other experienced women pilots, she received a telegram from Nancy Love and Base Commander Colonel Robert H. Baker, U.S. Army Air Forces.

Minus Western Union's standardized gibberish, here's what the telegram said:

> Ferrying Division Air Transport Command is establishing group of women pilots for domestic ferrying. [Within the United States and Canadian borders.] Necessary qualifications are high school education, age between 21 and 35, commercial license, 500 hours, 200 horsepower rating. Advise commanding officer 2nd Ferrying Group, Ferrying Division Air Transport Command, Newcastle County Airport, Wilmington, Delaware, if you are immediately available and can report at once at Wilmington at your own expense for interview and flight check. Bring two letters recommendation, proof of education and flying time.

Teresa now had 2,254 hours of flying time.

Chapter Four

New Castle Army Air Base

AS TERESA JAMES BOARDED the train for Wilmington, Delaware, she began her World War II journal. (Excerpts from Teresa's journal are italicized throughout this book.)

September 17, 1942:

En route from Pittsburgh, Pennsylvania: Here I am on my way and I still don't believe they will let us ferry airplanes for Uncle Sam!

Whereas, they have decided to let us try, be it resolved that come hell, high water and insulting criticism, we will not let Washington down. Amen!

September 18, 1942, 5:45 a.m.:

Hotel DuPont, Wilmington, I cannot sleep. I don't know whether this is a normal situation or not, but I do know that I am not reacting normally to it. I'm to meet two prospective WAFS [Women's Auxiliary Ferrying Squadron] in the Coffee Shop at 6:30. They can probably give me some pointers.

September 18, 1942, 10:00 a.m.:

Headquarters, New Castle Army Air Base—I rode out to the Base with Aline Rhonie and Helen Mary Clark. Helen Mary was encouraging, said I had nothing at all to worry about but I find myself afraid I'll be afraid.

The cabby stopped at the guard gate for clearance to drive us to a building called BOQ 14. [Bachelor Officer Quarters] He drove us up a three or four block long dirt road that had been graded but with no asphalt topping. He stopped in front of a two-story building and the guard who had accompanied us said "this is it."

I just looked!

There were planks where the steps should be. We had to walk across the planks to get into the BOQ. Well, we made it! It's a good thing I had only a little overnight bag. All I can remember was the miserable rain and mud, mud, mud!

Our new home was built from two by fours, planks and boards. One window per room, two if you had a corner room. I thought at that moment I had to be crazy for leaving my comfortable home and lucrative job as flight instructor. I never expected to see such a barren structure."

The men who had occupied BOQ 14 had moved to another building, and Teresa was expecting furnishings. She was wrong.

As I strode through the first floor, layered with mud, I passed the vacant rooms and was astonished at the sunlight peeking through the cracks in the walls.

I thought maybe the second floor might be better. I proceeded to the stairs in the rear of the building, climbing the 14 steps. I immediately picked out a room with the least daylight peeking through the cracks. One cot with sagging springs and an uncomfortable looking metal chair.

I left my bag in the room and reported to Onas P. Matz at the Operations Building across the mud puddles from BOQ 14. This is not at all what I had expected an Army Base to be. I don't know what I expected, probably old red brick buildings with ivy clinging all over. Matz told me the reason everything was knee deep in mud and otherwise under construction was that the base was new.

Matz told her to report to Lieutenant Joe Tracy for a flight check, and he told her how to get to the flight line.

I dodged backhoes, scrapers, bulldozers and stares from civilian heavy-equipment operators and wondered how I was going to scrape the mud off my shoes so I could work the rudder pedals.

My flight check is scheduled for 11. I hoped it would not be in that low-winged job I saw in the distance. Don't know where the nose rides on low wing airplanes."

Later that same day, Teresa wrote:

Well, the flight check was in the low-winged job. Lt. Joe Tracy checked me out. We took off and climbed to 2,500 feet. Did power stalls, 720-degree turns, lazy eights, chandelles, etc. [Chandelles and lazy eights are precision aircraft maneuvers.] Came back and landed and I began to wonder how everything had gone.

The lieutenant didn't say a word. He didn't look encouraging or discouraging. I was told to go to Headquarters, which I did. I sweated out a couple of eternities until Nancy Love came out and told me I passed. I felt very warm inside, but no use relaxing. The Board still has to pass me and then I have to take the Army physical.

Nancy Love is everything I thought and more! Beautiful, capable, charming. Wish she would show up right now. Twice she has put me at ease, and I could stand it again.

Later that same day in September 1942, Teresa noted in her journal things she was sure she would never forget from that first day:

The sensation of sitting on one side of a closed door while my destiny was being tossed about on the other side. Relief when Colonel Baker said I was accepted for training. The friendliness I saw registered in Adela Scharr's large eyes.

Late at night on that pivotal day of Teresa's life, she captured more of her experiences in her journal:

I wallowed through the mud to the sub-depot to draw out flying jacket, helmet, goggles, boots, coveralls. I never was sure of my size. Now I never will be. If those coveralls are size 36, I'm a size 13.

I look forward to knowing these girls better. From all appearances and conversations, I do not have any doubts. Met Betty Gillies, a wee person with the merriest blue eyes; Esther Nelson, a tall, pleasant girl who looked as if she had escaped from a page of Vogue; and Cornelia Fort.

Cornelia was instructing in Honolulu that fateful day the Japanese struck. After getting back on the ground with her student, they discovered a couple of bullet holes in the right wing of her airplane.

The BOQ was declared "ready" on September 18. The women could move in. Up until then, the earliest arrivals had been staying at a guest house called Kent Manor.

BOQ 14 consisted of forty-four square-shaped rooms, each with a cot, a straight chair, and a dresser. The only place to hang clothes was from a pipe between a pair of two-by-four boards. The latrine and shower facilities were definitely designed for men.

The particular BOQ—Bachelor Officer Quarters—where Teresa and the other women were staying was bare, to say the least. Here's what Teresa recorded in her journal:

We early girls got the "choice" rooms on the second floor of their barracks. But that night I realized I'd selected the wrong room. I'm across from the "bippy." Commodes flushing at all hours, singing in the shower.

And speaking of the bath facilities! No doors on the stalls! No curtains on the showers! I thought I'd die of embarrassment. I have so many personal hang-ups to overcome! Sitting on the commode while everyone is showering and putting on their makeup in front of that mirrored wall was a bit much.

Several of the girls didn't seem to mind it, but I found out later they were graduates of exclusive girls' schools. Turns out they were used to it.

As of September 21, 1942, ten women had gathered at New Castle Army Air Base: Nancy Love, Betty Gillies, Cornelia Fort, Aline Rhonie, Helen Mary Clark, Catherine Slocum, Adela Scharr, Esther Nelson, Teresa James, and Alma Heflin.

The women were issued standard U.S. Army khaki flight coveralls, a parachute, goggles, a white silk Army Air Forces scarf and leather flying jackets with the Air Transport Command patch.

WAFS headquarters was located in this building, New Castle Army Air Base, Wilmington, Delaware. First Nancy Love then—as of January 1943—Betty Gillies ran the squadron from there. *Courtesy Robert Patterson, grandson of Col. Robert H. Baker, 2nd Ferrying Group Commander 1942-43.*

The quartermaster supplied all this as well as cold-weather gear. Nothing the women received actually fit; everything was made for men. They had to make do.

These ten bold women stepped into history as the first members of the Women's Auxiliary Ferrying Squadron (WAFS) of World War II.

Nancy Love and Colonel Baker review the WAFS: from left, Betty Gillies, Esther Nelson, Cornelia Fort, Teresa James, Catherine Slocum, Del Scharr, Helen Mary Clark, and Aline Rhonie. *Courtesy: International Women's Air & Space Museum, Cleveland, Ohio*

Chapter Five

The Originals

"WHEN WE ALL ASSEMBLED in Wilmington, it was like we spoke different languages," said Gertrude Meserve, one of the potential new WAFS who arrived at New Castle Army Air Base in Delaware on September 30, 1942. "Florene with her Texas drawl, Nancy Batson and her even more leisurely Alabama drawl, Jamesy with her slangy Pittsburghese, me from Baahston."

Not only did their speaking styles vary, their backgrounds were vastly different. Cornelia Fort was the daughter of Nashville's Old South society. Evelyn Sharp had been raised by adoptive parents struggling through the Depression years in rural Nebraska.

Three were wives of men prominent in three different East Coast industries: Betty Huyler Gillies was married to Grumman Aircraft vice president Bud Gillies; Catherine Slocum to the publisher of the *Philadelphia Enquirer*; and Helen Mary Clark, whose husband, Gerould, headed an established New Jersey real estate business. All three women left children at home with fathers who were exempt from the draft for one reason or another. Catherine Slocum and Helen Mary Clark had capable nannies to help take up the load, and Bud Gillies' mother offered to help share the load of childcare.

Betsy Ferguson and Bernice Batten hailed from wheat farming communities of eastern Kansas; Adela "Del" Scharr was the daughter of a St. Louis police officer; Nancy Batson was the daughter of a Birmingham building contractor; and Teresa James was the daughter of a Pittsburgh florist. Aline "Pat" Rhonie was a divorcée who served with the British Red Cross Ambulance Corps in France before the Germans overran the country.

Most of the women had been employed in aviation as flight instructors. Dorothy Fulton and Esther Nelson ran airport flight services. Esther was also a qualified interior decorator. Pat Rhonie was an artist who painted aviation murals.

Del Scharr had her master's degree in psychology and had taught disadvantaged children in the St. Louis public schools. But when she married Harold Scharr, she was forced to quit, because the schools wouldn't employ married women as teachers. So Del, a fully qualified pilot by then, taught flying and ground school instead.

In age, they covered the allowed span—Helen Richards, the youngest had just turned twenty-one; Betty Gillies, Pat Rhonie, Del Scharr, and Lenore McElroy (who joined in January 1943) all were thirty-four. All had a minimum of 500 flying hours. Most had considerably more.

In World War II, everyone in the nation pitched in to shoulder his or her share. It was known as patriotism, and they were in it "for the duration." This group of women in the newly created Women's Auxiliary Ferrying Squadron (WAFS) came to be known as "The Originals." In January 1943, three more women were accepted and joined the initial twenty-five who had arrived in the autumn of 1942. Thus, the final number of "original" WAFS was twenty-eight.

This squadron of experienced women pilots, the first to fly for the U.S. Army Air Forces in World War II, proved their mettle in spades as America entered its second year of the war.

Once the press got wind of the fact that women were being hired to fly airplanes for the Army, New Castle Army Air Base was deluged with reporters and photographers and requests for interviews. This, it seemed, was the story of the century.

Nancy Love, a very private woman, was subjected to requests from press photographers for "cheesecake shots"—showing lots of leg or a bare shoulder—which she refused to do.

"No one had anticipated the heavy, widespread publicity," WAFS Delphine Bohn of Amarillo, Texas, wrote in her unpublished memoir *Catch a Shooting Star*. "The military was deeply affronted that this strange, multifaceted publicity could afflict them so. We were women looked upon as two-headed oddities. Everyone wished to examine each of us minutely. For some of us it was purely terrorizing."

Many of the stories written and disseminated were blatantly incorrect, grossly exaggerated, or just plain fabricated. The Army tried to protect the women from the spotlight, but they were not only in the bright glare of publicity, but under the microscope of public opinion as well. To their credit, not a word of scandal was ever connected with one of The Originals during the time they served Uncle Sam.

✠ ✠ ✠

Base Commander Colonel Robert H. Baker put out a memorandum on September 21, 1942. The WAFS would be designated Civilian Pilots. They would have all the privileges of officers including use of the Officers' Club and the Officers' Mess. They would stand formation and roll call along with the men at 8:00 each morning.

On September 23, the WAFS 30-day orientation began. Their curriculum included twenty-five hours of flight and seventy-two hours of ground school. All were experienced pilots—with 500 hours minimum—but they needed to learn to fly "the Army way!"

Flight instruction consisted of re-familiarization with standard flight maneuvers and cross-country navigation. (In this era before

GPS, air navigation meant relying on maps, compass readings, and landmarks.) Ground school, however, was a continuing process, made up of a review of communications, navigation, meteorology, how aircraft were powered, military forms, military law, and military drill.

When not out ferrying planes, all pilots—male and female—were expected to keep up to date on increasingly complex aircraft, advanced communications and instruments, and Link Trainer (instrument training) time.

Teresa's journal entries offer insight into these early days of the WAFS:

It looks as if the rains have come. For six days we haven't been able to fly.

New recruits from every section of the country. Helen Richards, southern California; Barbara Poole, Detroit; Gertrude Meserve, Boston; Barbara Erickson, Seattle; Florene Miller and Delphine Bohn, Texas; and Phyllis Burchfield, Pennsylvania. They are all starting where we started.

In late September 1942, she wrote:

Flying is flying, but Army flying is another story. When they tell you to make a 90-degree turn they don't want 89 or 91 degrees. "You've got to hit it on the nose, Sister, and I don't mean maybe!" is the instruction issued by the Army. We are used to the masculine attitude toward women and aviation, thank goodness!

Mrs. Anderson came to live with us. She is official housekeeper of our BOQ. She likes girls and flying. Plenty of both here. We like her, too—so much that she has already been designated as "Andy."

Colonel Baker decided that, once their uniforms arrived, the WAFS needed to take part in the base's Saturday Morning Review—a close-order drill. Nancy Love had designed the WAFS' gray wool uniforms, and they had been fitted by a tailor in the nearby town of Wilmington, Delaware. The WAFS, wearing their newly designed jackets, trousers, and overseas caps, were about to make their marching debut.

Nancy and her "girls" found themselves in for a challenge. Marching in formation certainly was not what they had signed up for.

"Nancy's inability to develop a loud-mouthed 'hup, two, three, four' Marine drill sergeant style was legend," Delphine Bohn wrote in *Catch a Shooting Star*. "It caused her to develop occasional mental lapses when we were drilling."

Nancy admitted her own inadequacy. "As Commander," she wrote, "I had to lead the formation and give the commands, which, because I was very self-conscious, was not one of my strong points. In fact, I so hated having to roar out orders that I occasionally drew a blank on what command to give next.

"This happened to me one dreary morning when we were drilling on an inactive runway. The squadron was marching smartly down the paved runway toward its end, where there was a sharp drop-off of about ten feet. Panic struck me as we approached the precipice, and I found myself incapable of giving the command, 'To the rear—march!'

"So off went all the girls, still in close formation and roaring with laughter. Straight down the embankment they went and into the field, leaving me standing at the top, still speechless."

Teresa's journal captures the excitement of joining the war effort—and becoming one of the first female pilots in the Army. On October 12, 1942 (Columbus Day), she wrote:

Again, we march. Poor Nancy! She is the one in line for sympathy, having to bear the brunt of our zigging when we should have been zagging.

We are standing on a newly paved runway watching the men pass in review this morning. They were just passing the stand when a B-24 and six P-38s took off for foreign territory and flew right over us. A goose pimple moment!

The mud doesn't matter. The continuous rain and cold don't matter. I'm just so proud to be here, to be a part of this Army. There's something a little difficult to describe about soloing a plane with a big star on it.

October 19:

We were graduated today. Eight of us! Nancy Love, Betty Gillies, Cornelia Fort, Aline (Pat) Rhonie, Helen Mary Clark, Del Scharr, Esther Nelson, and yours truly. Our cross country in PT-19s is finished. Can't wait for orders to deliver.

October 20:

Slept swell last night. Dreamed I was ferrying a bomber. Well, they didn't say we could, but they didn't say we couldn't either.

✜ ✜ ✜

"The Originals": The twenty-eight original WAFS (women selected to form the U.S. Army Air Forces Women's Auxiliary Ferrying Squadron)

25 WAFS in the order they joined, as of December 31, 1942:

1. Nancy Love
2. Betty Gillies
3. Cornelia Fort
4. Aline "Pat" Rhonie
5. Helen Mary Clark
6. Adela "Del" Scharr
7. Esther Nelson
8. Teresa James (nickname "Jamesy", married name Martin)
9. Barbara Poole (post-war married name Shoemaker)
10. Helen Richards (post-war married name Prosser)
11. Barbara Towne (post-war married name Dickson)
12. Gertrude Meserve (married name Tubbs, as of April 1944)
13. Florene Miller (post-war married name Watson)
14. Barbara Jane "BJ" Erickson (post-war married name London)

15. Delphine Bohn
16. Barbara Donahue (post-war married name Ross)
17. Evelyn Sharp (nickname "Sharpie")
18. Phyllis Burchfield (nickname "Burchie", married name Fulton)
19. Esther Manning (married name Rathsfelder, as of early 1943)
20. Nancy Batson (post-war married name Crews)
21. Katherine Rawls Thompson
22. Dorothy Fulton (post-war married name Slinn)
23. Opal "Betsy" Ferguson (post-war married name Woodword)
24/ Bernice Batten
25. Dorothy Scott

Three additional women joined the WAFS in January 1943:
26. Helen McGilvery
27. Kathryn "Sis" Bernheim (post-war married name Fine)
28. Lenore McElroy

Author's note: Alma Heflin McCormick began training but failed to achieve the necessary 200-horsepower rating. Catherine Slocum completed and passed all the requirements, but at the end of the women's training she returned home out of necessity. She had left four children at home with her husband and a nanny, but the nanny had fallen ill. Like Heflin, Slocum is not counted in the final number of "The Originals"—the first group of women to ferry planes for the U.S. during World War II. This is because neither woman ferried an airplane for the Air Transport Command's Ferrying Division.

Teresa "pulls the prop" to start an Army L-4B Piper Cub liaison aircraft. These planes did not have electric starters. The aircraft had to be started by "pulling the prop through." That means someone had to put both hands on the higher propeller blade and pull down hard (cranking the engine) and immediately stepping back out of the way of the blades as they caught and began to whir at a very rapid rate. It could be dangerous and one had to learn the correct timing and way to do it. Teresa mastered the technique. *Courtesy the International Women's Air & Space Museum, Cleveland*

Chapter Six

The First Ferrying Flight

THE WAFS MADE THEIR FIRST FERRYING FLIGHT October 23-24, 1942.

Nancy Love appointed her second-in-command Betty Gillies to lead the flight of six L-4B Cubs from the Piper factory in Lock Haven, Pennsylvania. The Cubs were liaison aircraft used by the Army for communication and coordination. They were small and maneuverable, able to land on grass, sand, or any bare ground.

The WAFS destination was Mitchel Field on Long Island, New York. Cornelia Fort, Helen Mary Clark, Aline "Pat" Rhonie, Del Scharr, and Teresa James made up Betty's crew for this mission.

Colonel Baker flew them to Lock Haven. The alternative was a four-hour train ride in the middle of the night, after which the women would have to arise at five in the morning in order to get off at their destination, the Piper factory.

Teresa's journal offers a blow-by-blow description of their two-day adventure:

We inspected our ships, climbed in and took off for Allentown, Pennsylvania. RONed—spent the night in a hotel there—two to a room. We had been thoroughly trained and familiarized with how to fill out the necessary RON [Remain Over Night] forms.

That night, Betty talked to her husband, Bud. He warned her that bombing practice was planned the following day in the area on

Long Island where they would be delivering their Cubs. All flying had been ordered grounded during the bombing. When she got up the next morning, Betty wired Mitchel Field Operations to let them know the WAFS were coming in with deliveries that morning.

"Please call off the guns until we can get the planes safely on the ground," she requested.

Teresa's journal continues the story:

We headed for Long Island. Betty, being familiar with the look of the greater New York area from the air, led the flight into Mitchel Field. It only took us sixty-five minutes.

Betty signed over the planes to a bad-tempered officer who told her—in no uncertain terms—that he needed them two months ago, not now!

"That's not my problem," she told him. "I'm merely following orders. You may speak to my commanding officer, Colonel Robert Baker at New Castle Army Air Base, or call Colonel Tunner himself at Ferrying Division headquarters."

She gave the man a big smile. We all knew that smile was delivered around clenched teeth.

About then the phone rang. It was the telegram Betty had sent asking them to call off the bombing until the Cubs were safely in. It was a couple of hours late being delivered.

Betty paled when she heard the news. But the Cubs were safely in, no thanks to either Western Union or Operations at Mitchel Field.

☆ ☆ ☆

A few weeks later on November 10, 1942, Betty Gillies, Cornelia Fort, Helen Richards, Barbara "BJ" Erickson, Barbara Poole, Barbara Towne, and Teresa James took seven Cubs south. Ferrying Cubs was not something that could be done swiftly. This airplane's fuel capacity was only twelve gallons. The 65-horsepower engine could average only 75 miles per hour. They had to make frequent stops to refuel.

The first PT-19 flight: Squadron leader Betty Gillies (left) leads Nancy Batson, Esther Nelson, Helen Mary Clark, Teresa James, and Evelyn Sharp on a flight south. *Courtesy: WASP Archive, Texas Woman's University Library, Denton*

The Cubs carried no radios and only minimal instrumentation, so they could not be flown in anything but good visibility, known as VFR (Visual Flight Rules). Consequently bad, even marginal, weather grounded plane and pilot indefinitely. Winter weather made day-to-day flying conditions for light aircraft highly unstable.

It became a standing joke among the women ferry pilots that while heading west across Ohio and Indiana, the cars going 60 miles an hour on U.S. 40 below were "passing" them.

The field at their destination, Charlottesville, Virginia, had been flooded and was a sea of mud. On landing, both Poole and Fort's aircraft tipped forward onto their propellers, damaging them. Richards landed safely but sank in up to her knees when she got out of her airplane.

Finally, on November 22, the WAFS were dispatched on their first PT-19 delivery. This was the airplane Colonel William Tunner had hired them to ferry. Teresa, along with Betty Gillies, Helen Mary Clark, Florene Miller, Barbara "BJ" Erickson, Evelyn Sharp, Nancy Batson, Esther Nelson, Helen Richards, Del Scharr, and Phyllis Burchfield were on their way to the Fairchild factory in Hagerstown, Maryland.

By late November the weather along the eastern seaboard was getting cold on the ground and colder aloft. Not only did the WAFS have to lug parachutes, because the PT-19s had open cockpits, they had to wear bulky winter flying gear.

They missed their bus in Baltimore by two minutes and, since there wasn't another one until seven in the morning, they had to sleep on benches in the station, propped against parachutes and B-4 bags, their military-issued suitcases. Their tardy arrival at the Fairchild factory in Hagerstown brought the wrath of the Army down on them.

"Where the h… have you been?" the captain in charge demanded. "Everyone in the Army has been looking for you."

Their explanations fell on deaf ears.

The next day, Thanksgiving Day, the WAFS crew turned their airplanes south, arriving in time to enjoy a turkey dinner with the men at Morris Field, Charlotte, North Carolina. The women spent the night in the nurses' BOQ.

Back on base in Wilmington just after midnight on November 28, they were off again the next morning. Same crew—Clark, Gillies, Burchfield, Nelson, Batson, Sharp, Miller, Erickson, Richards, and James—but back to the Cubs that Teresa calls "those Lock Haven spitfires!"

Colonel Baker, again taking pity, flew them up to Lock Haven in the C-60 transport, but weather closed in on them en route, and he had to fly by relying on instruments only. The rest of the way they flew looking out the window at soup. On the ground, it was snowing.

This time everybody was going in a different direction. "Jamesy" and "Burchie"—Phyllis Burchfield had acquired a nickname as well—headed for Vermont. It was November 30. They RONed that night in Albany, New York, where the ground was covered with snow. Fort Ethan Allen was their destination, and they arrived on December 1.

They caught an airliner headed for LaGuardia Field outside New York City and flew through a snowstorm to get there. "Couldn't even see the edge of the wings," Teresa relates. Jamesy and Burchie got to spend four hours in New York, time enough for dinner and a movie, before catching a late train out. They arrived back at the BOQ at 5:00 in the morning of December 2.

"Seven of us were in the BOQ that night," Teresa recalled. "The wind was blowing, and it really started to snow. Then Nancy Love called and said for us to pack, that we were on our way to Montana! Everyone went crazy with excitement."

Posing for the society editor of the Great Falls, Montana, newspaper: PT-17 ferry pilots Delphine Bohn, Nancy Batson, Kay Rawls Thompson, Florene Miller, Phyllis Burchfield and flight leader Teresa James. *Courtesy: WASP Archive, Texas Woman's University Library, Denton*

Chapter Seven

Destination: Great Falls, Montana

IN HER JOURNAL, Teresa continued to capture highlights of her WAFS adventures. Just a few days after arriving back at the BOQ, Teresa sensed that something was in the air. She recorded this entry on December 3, 1942:

Something is cooking! Something even bigger than the trip to Great Falls. Something else.

We all got up at six a.m. Everybody anxious and ready to travel. A mad house with all these females getting clothes ready with only one iron and three wash basins in the place. At two, Nancy called and told us we weren't going until tomorrow. She had to go to Washington.

Ah, hah!

They did not leave the next day because *Look* magazine came to do a story on the WAFS and take pictures of the nine women present on base. Posing together were Dorothy Fulton, Katherine Rawls Thompson, Betsy Ferguson, Florene Miller, Teresa James, Delphine Bohn, Dorothy Scott, Nancy Batson, and Phyllis Burchfield. Three of them, Ferguson, Fulton, and Scott, were still in the midst of their thirty-day orientation. The spread in the magazine—which ran in January 1943— was a "big deal" as it was the first such story the press was allowed to do on the women pilots serving at New Castle Army Air Base.

Teresa wrote that night:

The photographers captured all of us doing our regular work at the base. We never know what minute of the day or night we will be notified to leave. After eight hours of photographs, we were all ready for bed.
December 4, 1942:

Same old story! We were up and ready to travel at seven a.m. But—we didn't leave until the day was almost over AND after Nancy informed us that she wasn't going on the trip. She seemed very disappointed, and we felt sorry for her.

But like I said—something's going on. She's named me flight leader in her place.

Headed for Great Falls, Montana, with Teresa were Nancy Batson, Florene Miller, Delphine Bohn, Phyllis Burchfield, and Kay Rawls Thompson.

In her journal, Teresa's captures details of her crew's Great Falls adventure:

Thompson has been waiting for her husband—Captain Ted Thompson of the British Royal Air Force (RAF)—to get time enough off so she could see him. He called today and announced he would have four days. And we're getting ready to leave!

Even though her time was limited, she had dinner with him in Philadelphia, then they rushed back to Wilmington where we were to meet at the station at nine p.m. Honest, she was beaming like a Fourth of July sun, and who could blame her. Is he a handsome fellow or not? He rode with us to Pittsburgh on the train.

Twenty-seven male flying officers were going to Great Falls, Montana, with this WAFS crew.

The previous spring, the U.S. had sent thirty-three Stearman PT-17 trainers to the Canadian RAF for cadet flight training. But, like the PT-19s the WAFS had been flying, these airplanes had open cockpits. The winter weather in Alberta, Canada, was not conducive to open cockpit trainers, so the Canadians were returning them to Uncle Sam. The planes were destined for a flight training school located in the more temperate climate of Jackson, Tennessee.

So the WAFS and the flight officers boarded a train and began their transcontinental train ride from the East Coast to Great Falls, Montana.

December 5, 1942:

We were in a state of nervous collapse. Instead of the staterooms we had expected, we found that the six girls and twenty-seven men were to occupy one Pullman car. The berths were made up, so the only thing to do was go to bed. A lot of wisecracking accompanied this—like, "don't walk in your sleep!" One girl had a fellow in the berth above her. I don't think she took her clothes off the entire night.

Nobody slept well that night. The train was stopped for a long time, and it got very cold. One of the steam lines had burst, the reason for the frigid surroundings. The brakeman came around and told them they were running four hours late.

Once they were rolling again, most of the women spent the afternoon catching up on the sleep they'd missed the night before.

That evening the boys loosened up, told some jokes, and we did a bit of hangar flying [swapping flying stories while sitting in an airport hangar or elsewhere]. *They really treated us swell, gave us credit for being capable, most of the time, so we can't complain. Went to bed about 1 in the morning.*

December 6, 1942:

Got up around noon. They left six of the berths made up at the end of the car and we took turns napping. Sang all the old songs we knew. There is much joy in mass singing. The fellows played every card game imaginable—from poker on down. We pulled into Chicago at eight thirty p.m., three hours late, completely starved.

Miller, Batson and I, and three of the guys decided to go have dinner. We crowded about four days into that four hours.

This job has been mostly hard work and waiting and wondering, but we have our moments of "goose pimple" thrills and going into the Pennsylvania Station in Chicago and looking at that collection of airplane models there was one of those.

A model of every type of airplane was there, from P-38s, B-25s, B-24s on down to the training "ships" like the PT-17s and PT-19s— an exhibition of U.S. flying strength.

We walked and it was snowing. Traffic was slowed by it and we could reach out and pick handfuls off the cars. Naturally, we had a snowball fight. And we heard Christmas carols. We were in uniform and caught the eyes of hundreds of passers-by.

The following day, December 7, was not only the first anniversary of the attack on Pearl Harbor, it also happened to be Florene Miller's twenty-second birthday. The "gang" planned to get her a present and have a little party for her later, but no shops in the Chicago train station were open. They finally settled on a Santa Claus filled with Hershey's Kisses.

Back on the train, at midnight, they presented the card and gift to her and sang happy birthday.

We stayed up until five in the morning, singing and having a merry time. One of the lieutenants is falling in love with Miller. He follows her around the train with that look in his eyes.

December 7, 1943:

Nobody got up until late. We had nothing to do but sleep. We got into Great Falls. At noon. It was about five above zero and snow over everything.

An Army bus took the WAFS to the Hotel Rainbow. They had the rest of the day off, so they went out to the Officer's Club at Gore Field. While there, Teresa got called over to Base Operations. There, she found out that, because of the low temperatures predicted, they were to fly south and then east instead of flying east and then south as planned to their final destination of Jackson, Tennessee.

All six women went into town and had dinner. They met an officer who knew Del Scharr and another who knew Evelyn Sharp. Now they had "Hello's" to deliver to their fellow WAFS when they got back to base. Both Teresa and Phyllis Burchfield thought they were coming down with colds, so they all decided to go back to the hotel and go to bed.

December 8, 1942:

Slept until noon. Might as well. Up here, the sun doesn't come up until after nine. Not even daylight until eight thirty. We had breakfast in bed for the first time and really enjoyed it.

The society editor of the Great Falls newspaper came to the hotel with the Public Relations Officer and took pictures. Spent three or four hours with that, then we went ice skating at the Civic Center with some of the boys.

None of the group, with the exception of Yours Truly, had ever been on ice skates before. After all, Batson, Bohn, Miller and Thompson all come from somewhere down in y'all land. But before the evening was over, they all had made solo flights.

By then Teresa knew she was coming down with something. Probably the flu, because whatever it was, it was causing her to feel pretty sick.

December 9, 1942:

I'm sick. Burchfield is sick. Miller's beginning to feel sick. But we had to go to the airport to get checked out in the PT-17s. Most of us had never flown this particular primary trainer before, so we each made a couple of trips around the field.

Had dinner at the Officer's Club. Then one of the lieutenants took Miller and me back to town to see a doctor as we were feeling mighty low. The doc says stay in bed, that I have the flu. I don't dare see the Flight Surgeon for fear of being grounded for a week.

December 10, 1942:

The next morning, Teresa stayed in bed. She writes that she drank three quarts of orange and grapefruit juice, "'til it ran out my ears." The lieutenant called to see how she was.

December 11, 1942:

They all were up at 6:00 a.m. and out at the airport. And there, they waited. It was a nice day, clear, and on the warm side. Teresa felt terrible. So did Burchfield, and Florene said she didn't think she could fly that day. The captain in Operations told them if they didn't feel like it, not to go.

I was so sick, I didn't care if the whole Army threatened to be waiting at the next airport. I don't remember being that sick for a long time. I went back to the hotel and went to bed and the others went ice skating. They seem to have caught that fever.

I stayed in bed until four that afternoon then went to the public stenographer to have my journal notes typed before I get too far behind. As I came back to the desk for my key, I heard someone call my name. When my fever-impaired vision finally focused in the right direction, who should I see standing before me but Nancy Love. And with her were a colonel and two captains.

Teresa was embarrassed. There she stood, fully dressed, and the man behind the hotel desk had told Nancy that she was ill. Immediately, Teresa felt that, as flight leader, she appeared to be letting Nancy down.

But Nancy had other things on her mind, "Come up to my room while I get changed," she said. "I've got an hour, and I want to talk to you."

Teresa learned that Nancy was on a fact-finding trip with several Ferrying Division officers. They were visiting the six other ferrying squadrons checking on possible quarters for the women. The tight-knit WAFS were going to be split up.

Teresa got on the phone and rounded up the rest of the women. She told them Nancy was there in Great Falls and wanted to talk to them as soon as possible. An hour or so later they were all were assembled, including the officers with Nancy.

The Ferrying Division was forming women's ferrying squadrons at other ferrying bases around the country. Some of the WAFS were going to be assigned elsewhere. Others would remain in Wilmington. Nancy added that, eventually, the women now in training at Jackie Cochran's flight school down in Texas—established in November and known as the Women's Flying Training Detachment—would be joining them. Each of the women's squadrons would grow with the addition of the newly graduated women pilots.

We had been together just over three months and, already, we were being split up. I'd grown to like these girls. On one side, I was sorry to hear the news. On the other side, things were starting to get exciting.

The six WAFS and their six Stearman PT-17s in Amarillo, Texas: From left—Kay Rawls Thompson, Phyllis Burchfield, Nancy Batson, Delphine Bohn, Florene Miller and flight leader Teresa James. *From the Author's personal collection: The photo, signed by four of the six WAFS, was a gift from Nancy Batson Crews.*

Chapter Eight

Six Yellow Stearman PT-17s

THE AIRPLANES THE WAFS were scheduled to fly awaited them—yellow bi-wing PT-17 Stearmans with a single 225-horsepower engine. Nickname, "Yellow Peril."

The temperature on departure day in Great Falls, Montana, was hovering around zero. The six women eyed the open cockpits with considerable trepidation. Already accustomed to flying open cockpit PT-19s out of Hagerstown, Maryland, they were no strangers to that kind of aerial discomfort. There, the damp cold was chilly and penetrating. But here, the zero degrees Fahrenheit was compounded by the five-thousand-foot altitude at Great Falls.

To add to that, some of the time they would be flying in mountainous country with sharp, rocky ridges and few hospitable places to put an airplane down in an emergency. The terrain looked rough, and the women were uneasy about it. Still, they kept an "if the fellows can do it, so can we!" attitude.

One last problem they had to contend with: It was so cold the line crew had to heat the engine oil in order to start the engines on the Stearmans.

The WAFS, looking like giant overstuffed penguins in their winter flight gear, waddled to the flight line. Apprehensive barely describes their feelings at that moment. Even Texans Bohn and Miller, used to wide open spaces, were not accustomed to rugged high country like this. And the other four were from tamer surroundings east of the Mississippi River.

Getting into the Army-issue, bulky winter flying gear was a challenge. The first layer consisted of long, scratchy woolen underwear and layers of socks. Over the long johns, they pulled on high-waisted, fleece-lined leather pants. These zipped from the shinbone of one leg up to the sternum and were held in place by suspenders.

Fleece-lined leather jackets topped all that. Leather flying caps with chin straps and goggles, fleece-lined leather gloves, and wool-lined boots completed their standard flying garb.

"We thought, surely, all this would be enough to keep the cold out, but it wasn't," Nancy Batson recalled. "To that, we added our parachute, with straps over the shoulders and around the thighs."

For the flight out of Great Falls, the women also received chamois [soft leather] masks held in place by wide black elastic bands. The masks were to provide at least some semblance of protection against frostbite since they would be flying another few thousand feet above the earth where the air was even colder. The WAFS already had learned, when flying in open cockpit trainers back East, that a runny nose was a constant companion.

Finally, the morning of December 12, they took off and headed south. These primary trainers carried no radios. The pilots could not communicate with each other or call for help.

December 12, 1942, Teresa's journal:

This was a morning I'll never forget. Snow covered everything. The world was white. We couldn't make out highways or railroads or rivers. Even though the airplanes were yellow, they were hard to see. You couldn't see the airplane ahead of you if you were level with it.

Florene was navigating and, in accordance with the WAFS rules of group flying, leading the line of airplanes in a loose formation. Not far out of Great Falls, I noticed that the other aircraft were circling. I watched, then flew down and tried to straighten them out. Went back to my spot, but Florene kept circling, followed by the others. I don't think we flew ten miles straight. Finally, I had to find out what was going on.

There was no place to land in this rugged country, but finally, "by some miracle," Teresa noticed a small auxiliary airfield that had been plowed out. With exaggerated gestures—repeatedly pointing down—she signaled to the others. Eventually, they realized what she wanted.

It isn't easy to put an airplane down in a furrow and I had visions of a crack-up, but I had to get to the bottom of this. I landed and the others followed. Even though it was icy, we all got down. We also had to leave our engines running 'cause they'd never have restarted in that cold.

Teresa found out what the trouble was.

Florene had lost her maps twenty miles out of Great Falls. The wind caught them and tore them out of her hand and into the frigid air. She had given the standard "fishtail" signal for someone else to take over and lead the line of airplanes, but nobody saw it. So she flew on with only her compass and her watch to guide her until they spotted the remote field.

They were in a place called Lavinia, Montana, and, despite the lost maps and circling, they were only ten miles off course!

We took off out of there—everybody got out fine—and flew on to Billings, where we RONed. It gets dark early up here and there is no other place to stay within reaching distance.

Now I am beginning to realize the demands and the loneliness of command. I went to bed in a hand-wringing, hair-tearing mode while the other five go to a movie.

The crew left Billings, Montana, following their orders to continue flying south before flying east to their final destination of Jackson, Tennessee. On December 13, 1942, Teresa captured some of the many challenges of this ferrying flight in a brief note in her journal:

Today we stay close together, determined not to have the same trouble. We flew at ten thousand feet. Snow still covered everything. Landed at Casper, Wyoming, at two p.m. Stiff from the cold, we continued on to Denver's Lowry Field to RON. Thompson navigated this leg. We all had a little trouble flying at such a high altitude.

The crew checked into the Cosmopolitan Hotel in downtown Denver. Teresa called Dink. Miller and Bohn called their mothers. Both families would meet the incoming pilots at the airfield in Amarillo, Texas, the following day.

December 14, 1942:

Bohn wants to leave early. She's going "home." So we're up at five a.m. But thanks to trouble getting breakfast and other delays, we don't get off until five minutes of nine. Landed at Pueblo, Colorado, at five minutes after ten.

On their way south to Amarillo the WAFS had to fly over Raton Pass, the nearly eight-thousand-foot route over the Colorado-New Mexico state line. That meant flying the Stearmans at an altitude of ten thousand feet, and the engines kept cutting out on them! The only explanation they could come up with was the high altitude. Worse, given the rugged terrain below, each had her doubts she could have found a place to land if, in fact, they were forced to do so.

It was clear when we approached Amarillo, and I could see it for a long time before we got there. I thought about how happy Bohn and Miller were bound to be, getting so close to their families and home.

Bohn led us in and everyone followed. Miller's mother, brother and sister were there and Bohn's mother and stepfather. Bohn's folks gave us a reception and dinner at the Herring Hotel. The usual photographers were there. And a toastmaster. We were called on to tell something of our experiences and of our present duties."

December 15, 1942:

Got up early and called the airport to see if the ships were ready. They were to fix Batson's wheel, and repair the place in Burchfield's wing where a mechanic stuck his foot through the fabric covering. But the planes weren't ready.

December 16, 1942:

The six PT-17s finally were ready, but it was too late in the day to leave. Delphine, Nancy and Teresa were invited to a party that evening—three hours of dancing and fun. Late that night, Teresa wrote in her journal:

A bunch of really interesting guys, I really had fun for the first time since the trip started.

December 17, 1942:

But Teresa paid for it the next morning! After several attempts to wake the flight leader, unsuccessfully, her roommate Nancy Batson soaked a towel in ice water and applied it to the back of Teresa's head and neck. Teresa was instantly awake.

We took off right into the sun. I'd never flown east into that blazing ball of fire before. Nearly blinded me. The day was perfect. Air smooth as glass. Could see fifty miles.

I like the West. It's difficult to believe the level plains would make such dazzling patterns from the air. The colors of rose, green, purple, blue and gold remind you of a patchwork quilt. The Red River was dry as a bone.

We were on our way to Love Field, Dallas. They say Dallas is the most cosmopolitan thing between New York and Frisco. Had a tail wind, so breezed right in. Ran into Erickson, Poole, Manning and Donahue there. They were getting out of PT-19s.

The crew RONed in Dallas, Texas, that night.

December 18, 1942:

The planes wouldn't be ready until 1:00 p.m., so they all slept 'til noon. Then they made a mad dash to the airfield, where they ran into Esther Nelson's husband.

Flew at three thousand feet coming into Longview. I didn't know there were so many oil wells. From a distance they resemble tall silver poles. Arrived Shreveport at five thirty. Batson and I both hit the sack. She had tonsillitis. I wasn't much better. I coughed away half a lung. Had trouble sleeping.

The next day, December 19, weather and bad luck conspired against the six WAFS. Visibility at the Shreveport, Louisiana, airport was poor. But when they finally were ready to take off, Florene Miller hit a field marker with her prop. She didn't do any damage, but they had to have the prop balanced. By the time it was fixed, it was too late to leave.

The next day the weather closed in and stranded the crew in Shreveport for three more days. By then, they were all broke. With their cash supply at a critical low, they couldn't go anywhere or buy anything. December 23, 1942:

Finally! By noon the weather cleared. Side light to feminine allure. There were six mechanics helping Miller into her flying suit while the rest of us struggled into ours alone. Landed in Little Rock. Batson is excited because her boyfriend—"the one"—is going to meet her in Nashville. Incidentally, the boys in Shreveport called her the Veronica Lake of the Ferry Command. [Veronica Lake was a 1940s movie star famous for her long, blond hair.]

December 24, 1942:

The day before Christmas and here we are. Everyone is so damned unhappy, it's a shame. We all had hoped to eat Christmas dinner at the base in Wilmington. At least we would have felt more at home. We are all really down in the mouth. Funny how at Christmas your thoughts turn to home. You just don't take Christmas Eve like all the other days. Still, we really don't have a thing to gripe about. After all, we are here in the good old U.S.A.

Teresa's journal tells us how the WAFS crew celebrated Christmas that year in Little Rock, Arkansas:

Miller called her boyfriend, and he is on his way here. Batson contacted hers in Nashville and he is on his way here, too. Poor fellow, he will be worn out. We got dressed and went walking, looking for a nice place to eat. There are hundreds of enlisted men here. Many of them saluted us, and we gave them a snappy one back.

We grabbed a streetcar to the station to meet Miller's boyfriend. The train was due at eleven, but it was two hours late. Took another car back to town. Went to Midnight Mass at St. Andrew's. With the bright lights, holly and decorations, this was the first real spirit we had felt.

Had to leave at twelve forty-five to meet the train. Back to the hotel and the party started in Miller's room and lasted until four a.m. The fog was terrible. You couldn't see across the street.

Christmas Day, December 25, 1942:

Batson's boyfriend arrived at five thirty in the morning. I dragged out at 11. Miller is out with her honey somewhere. I'm glad someone is happy today. All I can think about is how much I miss Dink, and how much I'd rather be with him right now.

Sat in the hotel coffee shop drinking eggnog and they informed us there was no more turkey or chicken. Who ever heard of a Christmas without turkey? We settled for pot roast.

The temperature in Little Rock was eighty degrees. They decided to take in a movie, *The Palm Beach Story*. Then, by some miracle, they found some turkey and had a late Christmas dinner. Teresa was in bed at 10:00 that night.

December 26, 1942:

Got clearance about ten thirty in the morning and took a crack at getting to Memphis. Only had a thousand-foot ceiling [the vertical distance from ground to cloud cover]. *Had fun flying in and out of the clouds. Thompson was navigating.*

They landed in Memphis, Tennessee, right on time and went into Base Operations. Thunderstorms surrounded Memphis, so they couldn't go on. Teresa called an old friend, Don, who was stationed there. He and his wife, Anne, invited Teresa and her friends out to the house for the day. Teresa spent the night with her friends.

December 27, 1942:

Rained all day. Stayed at Don and Anne's.

December 28, 1942:

Couldn't sleep. Weather still bad. Don said to call the other girls at the hotel and invite them out for a spaghetti supper. Took the girls back to the hotel at two thirty a.m. after a midnight snack at a popular Memphis eating place. Crawled in bed at 4 a.m.

December 29, 1942:

This is really getting to be funny now. Everywhere we stop, we sit for at least three days. There hasn't been any flying at all out of Memphis except by the airlines. It's a good thing I have good friends here. I only had fifteen cents when I hit town.

It looks like we will be going home on an airliner New Year's Eve—maybe. All we do is wonder from one day to the next.

December 30, 1942:

Nancy Love called Florene Miller to tell her that she was to return to Wilmington immediately. Nancy was on her way to be stationed at Love Field in Dallas. She would be taking Florene and three other WAFS with her to start up a new women's ferrying squadron there. Florene had to leave on the first available east bound airliner.

Teresa wrote:

I was a mite on the sad side when she left. Felt as if I were losing my best friend, but that's the Army. You meet people, become attached to them, and then you're transferred. Batson, Bohn, Miller and I had hoped that we would be together for a while. Miller promised she'd write me. I was feeling mighty low.

December 31, 1942:

The remaining five WAFS crew, along with one male pilot flying Florene's Stearman, didn't get away from Memphis until after noon because of the low ceiling. Then, big sigh of relief, they got off and delivered the ships to Jackson, Tennessee, their final destination.

They were met with, "Well, did you finally get here?" But, as of yet, none of the men flying the other 27 Stearmans had showed up.

Turns out we beat all the men in! Yep. Out of twenty-seven guys and six gals, we are the first ones to arrive out of that whole contingent that left Great Falls what seems like ten years ago. How 'bout these gals!

Don flew up to Jackson to bring us back to Memphis. After dinner with Don and Anne, the five of us said goodbye and left for the airport. We caught the American Airlines flight out of Memphis.

One of the loveliest scenes flying is skimming over the clouds with the moon shining on them. It's like looking at silver balls of cotton. It's an awesome sight regardless of how many times you see it. Happy New Year!

Then coming into Washington, D.C., I watched the sun come up. It's one of those moments that make you feel it's great to be alive!

January 1, 1943:

The next to final leg was via train. They got off in Philadelphia at 10:00 a.m. Teresa writes:

Got careless with Bohn's money and took a cab from Philadelphia to the base—cost thirteen dollars—but we were so tired we were dragging.

Went galloping through the BOQ hollering "Happy New Year." The gals and Mrs. Anderson gave us a royal welcome. Hugging, kissing, gee, it was just like coming home to your own family. Gillies and Clark joined Batson, Bohn and Thompson in my room, and we talked about what all was going on.

Got all the dirt. The second women's squadron being formed at Love Field in Dallas consists of Nancy Love, Helen Richards, Florene Miller, Dorothy Scott and Betsy Ferguson. They are going immediately. That's why Miller was called back. But she's still here going out of her mind checking in all her equipment, packing and so on.

More news! With Nancy moving on to Texas, Betty Gillies is our new boss. Also, Pat Rhonie resigned today. We're sorry to see her go.

Finally got to open my mail and my Christmas packages. Dink's letters are piled high. By ten p.m., that uncomfortable old cot looked mighty good. What a day! I just told Batson, I can't be this happy. Probably going to get hell somewhere along the line tomorrow. Hope not!

Ferrying high wing trainers south are five of the first 14 to qualify for the WAFS: kneeling, Teresa James #8 and Betty Gillies #2. Standing: Barbara Towne #11, Helen Richards #10, and Barbara "BJ" Erickson #14. *Courtesy the International Women's Air & Space Museum, Cleveland*

Chapter Nine

Twenty-eight Women Qualify as WAFS

TWENTY-FOUR WOMEN made up the Women's Auxiliary Ferrying Squadron as 1943 dawned.

Aline "Pat" Rhonie had been the fourth woman to qualify for the squadron. She enlisted for the initial ninety-day period—as did everyone—and did some ferrying between October 22 and late December 1942. She left at the end of December following a clash with base commander Colonel Baker. Rhonie is counted as one of the original WAFS, because she actively ferried aircraft before she left.

In January 1943, three more women—Kathryn (Sis) Bernheim, Helen McGilvery, and Lenore McElroy—joined the squadron, bringing the final official count of the Original WAFS to twenty-eight.

Betty Gillies and the New Castle Army Air Base review board accepted Bernheim and McGilvery after they passed their flight checks early in January 1943. Immediately, they began the thirty-day Army orientation at the base in Wilmington, Delaware. Later in the month, McElroy joined the 3rd Ferrying Group stationed in Romulus, Michigan.

McElroy was the mother of three teenagers, the wife of a Romulus ferry pilot, and a flight instructor. She had been flying for fifteen years and had 3,500 hours. Because of her children, McElroy had not been able to come to Wilmington in September. But with the establishment of a women's squadron in Romulus, McElroy applied. Nancy Love checked her out personally while visiting Romulus in mid-January. McElroy was accepted.

With those final three in the fold, The Originals were intact and ready to go into the history books as the first women's squadron to fly military airplanes for the U.S. Armed Forces. With Rhonie gone, the squadron now numbered twenty-seven.

In December 1942, when Nancy Love traveled to the other bases that housed ferrying groups, locating bed and board for the women while on base was her major concern. Willingness by the base commander to have women on base was another critical factor.

A decision was reached—new WAFS units would be established with the 5th Ferrying Group at Love Field in Dallas, Texas; the 3rd Ferrying Group at Wayne County Airport in Romulus, Michigan (near Detroit); and the 6th Ferrying Group at Long Beach, California. The 6th, with a majority of the aircraft factories building war planes located nearby, was the largest with four male ferrying squadrons already stationed there.

There were seven ferrying bases in all. The 2nd, the 3rd, the 5th, and the 6th would now host squadrons of women ferry pilots.

Nine WAFS squadron members would remain in Wilmington with Betty Gillies in charge. That women's ferrying squadron already was well established and actively ferrying aircraft. Five women each were sent to the three new squadrons.

Nancy Love knew she would be busy getting the Romulus and Long Beach squadrons up and running over the next few weeks, so she named Florene Miller to run the Dallas squadron. She named Del Scharr to lead the WAFS squadron in Romulus. Phyllis Burchfield, Barbara Poole, Barbara Donahue, and Kay Rawls Thompson went with Del, and Lenore McElroy joined them there. Then Nancy named Barbara "BJ" Erickson squadron leader of the

Long Beach WAFS. Going to California with "BJ" were Cornelia Fort, Barbara Towne, Bernice Batten, and Evelyn Sharp.

Teresa, Gertrude Meserve, Nancy Batson, Esther Nelson, Esther Manning, Delphine Bohn, Dorothy Fulton, and Helen Mary Clark remained in Wilmington under Betty Gillies' command. The two newcomers, Helen McGilvery and Sis Bernheim, brought the squadron count to 11.

Weather grounded much of the flying out of New Castle Army Air Base in January and into February. Then on February 16, 1943, Betty Gillies told Teresa that she had been selected to ferry a PT-19 from Hagerstown, Maryland, all the way to Burbank, California— coast to coast—all by herself. Teresa nearly came unglued. Dink was out in Southern California. After all these months, she would get to see him!

This was no ordinary ferrying trip. Teresa's assignment was to deliver the airplane to the famous flyer Major Paul Mantz. He was scheduled to fly it doing stunt work in the new film, *Ladies Courageous*. The movie was to portray the story of the WAFS. It starred Loretta Young as Nancy Love.

Teresa's assignment was a BIG first. A woman ferry pilot was to deliver an airplane from the East Coast to the West Coast. And she was going alone. Teresa possessed a sharp sense of history. She knew this was important.

Betty Gillies and Nancy Love knew their women pilots well by then, both their capabilities and their personalities. Assigning the Hollywood duty to the ultimate extrovert, Teresa James, was a stroke of genius. Always friendly, never at a loss for words, Teresa greeted life with a smile on her face. She had a good time wherever she went, and she looked good in her uniform. And she was quite attractive even though her looks were not of movie star quality like raven-haired Florene Miller or blonde Nancy Batson.

Besides, Teresa was long on experience. She could fly anything!

So at 12:30 p.m. on February 18, 1943, Teresa James, dressed in winter flying gear, her parachute bumping the backs of her legs, strode to the flight line amidst popping flash bulbs. She climbed into her PT-19 in Hagerstown and took off for the West Coast.

Her trip to Burbank took eight days. She could only fly during daylight hours and, typically, the open-cockpit aircraft fell victim to fog and bad weather en route. By Ferrying Division standards in early 1943, eight days wasn't at all bad for 3,000 miles. And gregarious Jamesy had a ball in spite of delays.

Teresa met and talked with friendly male pilots all the way across the south to Dallas. She flew with them when they were going her way and left them in her dust when they weren't. She never lacked for dinner companions at the bases where she stopped—usually male, but sometimes female as she ran into some of her fellow WAFS en route.

Teresa's early years as a stunt pilot and, more recently, her experience with long-distance ferrying missions gave her the confidence to fly solo across the continent. Plus, knowing she would be handing off her PT-19 to a famous Hollywood flyer was exhilarating! The icing on the cake, of course, would be the chance to spend time with Dink. But it wasn't just about the destination—getting there was half the fun! Here are excerpts from Teresa's journal between February 18 and March 11, 1943:

I'm going part way with six lieutenants. Gassed up in Lynchburg then went on to Charlotte. Had a lot of fun trying to fly formation with the six Looies. They sure are good. My nerves got the best of me, so I gave it up. They held the formation all the way to Charlotte, then peeled off into landing formation. Beautiful!

Fogged in early the next morning, but finally got off. Went to Atlanta where we landed to check the weather. It's very hazy. Could hardly see. I'm really having fun flying formation with these former cadets.

We decided to go on to Birmingham. What a town! It's so smoky you can't see a half mile ahead of you. Talk about Pittsburgh. It can't hold a candle to Birmingham. We kept circling at four hundred feet. Finally found the airport.

Teresa spent that night in the Nurses BOQ at another new Army base.

Had dinner in the Officers' Mess with Helen Richards' boyfriend— the one who sent her roses. Not bad looking.

The next morning, Teresa couldn't see the field for the smoke. Finally, she and her male pilot friends got out of Birmingham at 1:20 p.m. She wrote: "We had ever so much fun flying to Jackson, Mississippi. Zoomed all the towns.

It's Saturday night! Even the YW [YWCA] and the YM [YMCA] are filled up. Finally got a room at the Nurses' Quarters on base. Went dancing. The Royal Netherlands Army and Navy Air Force were training there. Danced with several of them. I got back to the Nurses' Quarters at 4 a.m.

Next morning, the airport was on instruments. Going nowhere today. Met some more of the Dutch boys and one of their American instructors who learned to fly with Batson. Another "hello" to deliver.

The next morning, Teresa and her new lieutenant pilot friends headed for Shreveport. She wrote:

Two of the Looies dropped down to ten feet over the ground. One zoomed a train. That started me off. I flew about fifteen feet over the highway scaring the hell out of everyone. Then I followed the train track for fifty miles. Headed straight for a train, then hopped up over him. I expected the engineer and fireman to leap right out of the cab.

Then I went and pestered the farmers. Scattered them in every direction. Boy, what a rip-roaring time I had. Good thing there are no numbers on the ships. [Numbers on airplanes are for identification. But, if someone on the ground "got a tail number" off of a plane doing supposedly forbidden aerobatic maneuvers in the air, they could report it. The pilot would be in considerable hot water in that case.]

After lunch, I left the boys and shoved off alone for Dallas.

When she had landed in Dallas and secured the airplane for the night, Teresa called the WAFS BOQ to see who was there. She learned that Nancy Love was in Washington and that Florene Miller and Dorothy Scott left on a trip a few minutes before she landed.

Richards and Ferguson were there. So spent hours chewing the rag with them. They have lovely quarters and raved about the base. I wish I was stationed here.

Next morning left Dallas for Abilene. Saw nothing but cattle, sagebrush and waterholes. Gassed up and went on to Midland. Lots of oil wells. Met a friend of Delphine Bohn's. Another "hello" to deliver.

Flew over Miller's hometown, Odessa. I don't like the dust. The wind was blowing about thirty-five miles an hour and I really bounced around. On my way to Pecos, came across this big army base. Landed amidst a flock of B-17s. They asked me for my clearance.

Teresa learned that she had landed at the wrong base. She was in Pyote, Texas. Pecos was twenty miles west.

They didn't have a flight plan on me and no wonder.

She realized she hadn't been watching the time. By accident, she had landed at the base occupied by the famous 19th Bombardment Squadron that already had blasted the Germans.

Nearly everyone here has been across several times. [To the war in Europe.]

Teresa left the next morning at 10:30, but had a tough time getting out. It was the first time a "girl flyer" had been on that base, and all the guys kept asking her questions. Finally, she headed for El Paso. The scenery was spectacular.

The sun shining on the Apache and Sierra Diablo Mountains is a beautiful sight. I feel so all alone up here. Nothing but vast space. I could see Guadalupe Pass for miles and miles. The mountains are several different colors—red, green, tan, brown and beige. I'm simply awed by the scenery.

I flew the borderline of the United States and Mexico—separated by the Rio Grande River, which looked like a narrow stream to me. Flew with one wing in Mexico and the other in the U.S. Crossed over the river at Fabens just to say I flew in Old Mexico. Had dinner at the Officers' Mess with one of the captains. He showed me the base and took me to look at El Paso and Juarez.

Flying from El Paso to Columbus, New Mexico, is strictly desert for seventy miles. Then on to Tucson. Desolate country. Not a check point for miles. I'd hate like hell to have a forced landing here.

Teresa did have trouble getting a room in Tucson, Arizona, but a colonel and his wife came to her rescue. He called the Nurses' BOQ and talked to the head nurse who gave Teresa a room. She had breakfast with the head nurse the next morning and then headed for Phoenix and, beyond that to Blythe, California.

That is by far the most desolate one hundred fifty miles I have flown! Nothing but airway light beacons for checkpoints. Left at 3:30 on my way to Riverside, California. More desert. Passed close to the Salton Sea, two hundred forty-five feet below sea level. Chocolate Mountains to my left. Straight ahead, San Jacinto Peak. It's covered with snow although the sun is very hot now.

I never knew there were so many mountains in California. I've never been this far west!

I'm going through San Gorgonio Pass and what a picture. When you start through it, you are about five hundred feet. Palm Springs is nestled at the foot of the San Gorgonio Mountains and the beginning of the pass. It gradually slopes upward to 1,963 feet. March Army Airfield is located at the top.

When she landed a Recon car [ground transportation provided to the pilots] picked her up and took her into Riverside. En route, she asked to stop and pick some oranges and lemons off of trees. She called Dink that night.

Was so excited, I couldn't sleep. Next morning headed for Burbank. Flew over Esther Nelson's home at Ontario and over the Rose Bowl in Pasadena. I delivered the ship to Paul Mantz.

Teresa's cross-country ferrying adventure was complete. Now, another adventure awaited—meeting famous Hollywood stars!

Teresa James heads for Hollywood in an open-cockpit, PT-19 trainer that is destined for the movies. *Courtesy: International Women's Air & Space Museum, Cleveland*

Chapter Ten

Teresa Takes Hollywood by Storm

AFTER DELIVERING THE PT-19 to the famous flyer Major Paul Mantz, Teresa met Loretta Young, the movie actress who was playing Nancy Love in the movie *Ladies Courageous*, supposedly about the WAFS.

From there, she got a C-78 ride over Hollywood, Los Angeles, and Santa Barbara right up the coastline. She spent February 27-28, 1943, with Dink in Santa Maria.

The next day, she was back in Burbank to catch the 2:40 a.m. train out. Teresa's journal captures her exciting, whirlwind activities in Hollywood, where she met many of the most famous, most glamorous movie stars of the day:

"*Major Paul Mantz wants to take me around to some of the studios. He gets me a room at the swankiest hotel on the West Coast. The manager is thrilled at having a girl flyer there.*

March 2 met band leader Ted Lewis. Walter Huston, Katie Hepburn, Spencer Tracy [movie stars] *are staying here. Spencer Tracy came over to the table. Went to the set of the movie Stormy Weather. Then on to the Palladium where Benny Goodman* [clarinet virtuoso and orchestra leader] *was playing. Topped off the evening at Romanoff's* [famous restaurant].

Went to Warner Brothers Studio and the set of the film Saratoga Trunk. *Met Ingrid Bergman and Gary Cooper* [movie stars]. *Talked with Gary for an hour. Back to the Brown Derby* [famous restaurant] *for dinner, where I was asked to join Bob Hope* [famous comedian and actor] *who was having dinner.*

I was thrilled to pieces. He invited me out to the Paramount Studio. Went on to the Coconut Grove at the Ambassador Hotel. Freddy Martin and his orchestra were playing. Met Freddy and, as usual, got questions about the uniform. I've caused no less than a sensation every place I've gone.

Teresa was introduced to songwriter Jimmy McHugh. He had just written Coming In On a Wing and a Prayer, for the movie by the same name.

He's sending me a copy. Then he introduced me to Ginny Simms [singer and actress]. *Wow, was I ever taken off my feet. She asked me if I could get an extended leave so I could appear on her Philip Morris program as guest star. Back at the hotel, I sent a telegram to Betty asking for a four-day extension.*

Telephone woke me from a sound sleep the next morning. It was the answer to my telegram granting leave permission.

The press wanted a photo of Teresa with Barney Ross, the lightweight boxing champion of the world. Ross, now in the U.S. Marine Corps, was just back from Guadalcanal in the Pacific theater of the war, where he had performed heroically in battle.

Had lunch with Ginny Simms and her mother, then dashed out to Paramount to meet Bob Hope. Went to the set of Lady in the Dark *where I met Ginger Rogers. She is one sweet girl. Met Warner Baxter, Veronica Lake, Paulette Goddard and George Reeves. Bob introduced me to everyone, calling me Jessie James, his little WAF. Met Eve Arden and dear sweet ZaSu Pitts. Met Mary Astor that night.* [All movie stars.]

The next morning she called Dink to tell him she WAS NOT back in Wilmington as he thought, but still in California. She told him she was coming up the next day to spend March 6-7 with him. To do this, Teresa had to forego a date to see Bob Hope in his radio show as well as a broadcast on which she was scheduled to appear.

Everyone thought I had run out on them. I just wanted to spend some quality time with my husband!

On March 8, she had dinner at the Brown Derby with Ginny Simms and her mother. She had received a telegram from the women back in Wilmington, excited to hear Teresa's radio interview with Ginny Simms. It read:

> ALL ELECTRICAL WIRING HAS BEEN
> CHECKED BY BASE ENGINEERING.
> NEW ANTENNAS ARE INSTALLED.
> AUDITORIUM ENLARGED.
> AWAITING THE HOUR.
> GIVE 'EM THE WORKS.

They were all gonna listen to the show. Ginny went over the script with me. We went on. That was, without a doubt, the longest five minutes I ever spent. Later, went back to the Brown Derby for dinner with the cast from the show, then they took me back to the studio for the big surprise.

They had made a recording of the show and we sat there listening to ourselves. The evening wasn't over until I got back to the hotel at two in the morning. I met so many people, I couldn't begin to remember their names. Everyone was swell to me.

But Little Cinderella goes back home tomorrow!

At the airport, people are staring at me like I'm a freak. This uniform attracts more attention. Major Mantz comes and keeps me company waiting for my airliner to leave.

✢ ✢ ✢

Thursday, March 11, Cinderella arrived back at Wilmington aboard a pumpkin. Found a "welcome home" sign in my room and a pile of mail, but I was too tired to open any of it. All the gals went on a trip to Canada. So to bed I go. I'm weary!

Author's note: Teresa's adventures in Hollywood certainly weren't the norm for the WAFS, but her own words written in her journal point to the hunger and willingness of celebrities and other civilians to treat World War II's men and women in uniform very well.

March 11, 1943, marks the end of Teresa's surviving diary. The rest was lost when the basement of her parents' home in Pittsburgh flooded several years later. The family threw out the soggy mess because it was unrecognizable as anything worth keeping.

It is our loss not to have Teresa's spirited take on the rest of her active duty with the WAFS. The rest of this book is based on the author's extensive 1999 and 2000 interviews with Teresa, and on many excerpts from the author's first book, *The Originals: The Women's Auxiliary Ferrying Squadron of World War II*.

Much of my source material comes from the WASP Archive at Texas Woman's University Denton. This includes material collected by others through interviews and oral histories done with Teresa. Additional sources are letters written by Teresa, articles written by her and about her, personal notes passed on to the author from other WAFS, and the first biography of Teresa, *On Wings to War: Teresa James, Aviator*, by Jan Churchill.

And may I add that Teresa was a huge help to me in writing *The Originals*.

Now, on with Teresa's story.

Chapter Eleven

Yes, the WAFS Will Fly Fighter Aircraft

IN THE EARLY MONTHS OF 1943, Nancy Love had other problems to contend with. She could see the handwriting on the wall. Jacqueline Cochran had succeeded in getting her flight training school set up in Texas. Already nearly 100 women pilots were in Houston learning to fly "the Army way." And more were arriving every month like clockwork.

Nancy didn't think Jackie would stop there and let something she had built slip easily away into another's—namely Nancy's—hands. Nancy also knew that Jackie had top U.S. Army Air Forces General Hap Arnold's ear, consequently, she was apt to get anything she asked for.

The WAFS future was going to change. Nancy was trying to make it as advantageous as possible for her women pilots. Already she had urged Colonel Tunner to let her and Betty Gillies check out in (qualify to ferry) bigger, more complex aircraft. He gave them the green light. Nancy was looking ahead at how and where the WAFS could be the most useful. She knew that transitioning up in aircraft complexity and size was a necessity if they were to keep their jobs and be of any real use to the U.S. Army Air Forces.

Early on, Colonel Tunner had identified the best approach to making ferry pilots out of men who already knew how to fly.

WAFS will fly fighter aircraft: Above — P-51 Mustang; Right — P-47 Thunderbolt, aka "The Jug". *Both photos courtesy: National Museum of the United States Air Force*

His goal was to qualify every male pilot in the Ferrying Division to ferry the biggest planes in the U.S. Army Air Forces—the four-engine bombers and cargo planes. He needed men capable of flying these bombers and fully loaded cargo planes across oceans, deserts, and mountains all over the world.

The men knew how to fly, but Colonel Tunner needed them to learn how to ferry all types of aircraft. The reason? Potentially a man—like the women pilots later on—could be called on to ferry a different aircraft every trip.

Colonel Tunner began by first putting the men in small single-engine primary trainers. They flew them cross-country, delivering these aircraft to their specific destinations. As they acquired the necessary know-how and experience, the men's instructors let them transition up and deliver intermediate-sized trainers, and then larg-

er advanced trainers. This way, the men gradually gained the confidence, experience, and skills necessary to be a ferry pilot for all types of aircraft.

When the time came to train women, it was obvious what worked for the men surely could work for the women pilots as well.

But that, in turn, created another problem.

If the Ferrying Division allowed its women ferry pilots to fly all of the small airplanes at the bottom of the transition ladder, the men who needed to begin at that level in order to work their way up would be denied that critical initial training.

This would negate the Ferrying Division's prime training strategy of getting male pilots ready to ferry the biggest bombers. Eventually changes would be necessary. Now they needed women to be qualified to ferry the smaller but powerful, single-engine, single-seat fighters—

also known as pursuits—across the country. Women who couldn't qualify to do that would no longer be needed.

Colonel Tunner knew the women pilots had great potential, but in the dreary, fog and ice-bound winter of early 1943, the WAFS barely were able to get their putt-putt airplanes off the snow-covered ground. It was up to the WAFS to gut it out and fly whenever the weather permitted. And so they did. Spring was coming.

Colonel Tunner had stationed the WAFS squadron at New Castle Army Air Base in Wilmington, Delaware, because it was located close to the manufacturers of small primary trainers (PT-19s) and even smaller liaison airplanes (L4-Bs—Cubs). Those were the two types of airplanes he initially hired the women to fly.

The women could and did handle these assignments well.

Then as the war moved further into 1943, the Army's needs, as predicted, began to change. The factories began retooling to build war planes—bigger, heavier, faster aircraft—particularly fighter planes like the P-47 and P-51 and twin-engine attack bombers like the A-20. By mid-summer 1943, this transition was well underway.

Now the Ferrying Division needed pilots who could fly these bigger, more powerful aircraft.

On January 15, 1943, the flight training school in Texas, initiated by Jacqueline Cochran and General Hap Arnold, was ready to welcome its third class. The first class was expected to join Nancy Love's ferrying squadrons that spring. The arrival of those women pilots would immediately double the number of WAFS. The second class of graduates would quadruple the number of WAFS.

That's why, in December 1942, the Ferrying Division had begun making plans to form WAFS units at three more bases.

Already, the original WAFS were itching to get their hands on the bigger stuff starting with the basic trainers (BT), advanced trainers (AT), and some assorted twin-engine craft. And Betty's women pilots had seen an occasional P-47 on the flight line at

Wilmington and watched the men take off in a roar. They wanted to get their hands on that airplane.

The factories producing these airplanes were scattered around the country, though the biggest concentration was in the Los Angeles Basin. The WAFS' potential for usefulness at other bases near these airplane factories was up for discussion. The distribution of women ferry pilots at bases around the country began.

Could the women fly these bigger, more powerful aircraft?

It was Nancy Love herself who provided the answer to that question.

Nancy had Colonel Tunner's OK to fly any airplane she thought she could handle. Her sights were set on the sleek P-51, the fastest of the single-engine pursuit aircraft. Pursuits were high-performance fighter aircraft with a seat for only one pilot. The first flight in a pursuit was a solo—no instructor on board.

Just as fledgling male P-51 pilots already had done, Nancy familiarized herself with the technical specifications of the P-51. Late in February 1943, at the end of an isolated runway at Long Beach, California, Nancy climbed into the P-51 Mustang. An instructor gave her a cockpit check and waved her off.

Nancy could not see over the massive engine in front of her. No pilot could. She "S-ed," or zigzagged, down the taxiway in order to see if there was anything blocking her way as she taxied the plane.

The moment of truth for any fledgling pursuit pilot comes when she sits, alone, at the end of the runway. The engine roars. She stands on the brakes to harness all that pent-up power and keep the aircraft grounded a few more seconds. Then Nancy released the brakes and shoved the throttle forward to the firewall. [The metal panel that separated the cockpit from the engine.]

The P-51, gathering all of its considerable power, surged forward. The tail lifted. Now Nancy could see straight down the runway. The wind caught under the wings, lifted the aircraft, and carried it swiftly up into the California sky.

The Mustang, she discovered, flew like any other airplane, only faster. The response to the stick and rudders was immediate and sweet. For an hour, she practiced maneuvers aloft. Then she began her descent, gradually bleeding off altitude until she was set up for her first landing. Moments later she was down and rolling along the runway.

When asked later about her historic flight, Nancy said, simply, that she felt "the same lonely but wonderful feeling you get on your first solo." Her instructor signed off in her logbook. "Qualified at Long Beach, Calif."

Now it was Betty Gillies's turn in the cockpit of a high-performance fighter aircraft.

On March 8, 1943, Betty wrote in her diary:

Today was clear but very windy and gusty. I flew the P-47 for one hour! Took off at 11:20, played around upstairs for 30 minutes and then shot two landings. Got it back all in one piece! Sure did get a kick out of it and it sure did keep me busy!

Betty Gillies was the first woman to fly the P-47 and Teresa's turn was coming!

Chapter Twelve

Seven WAFS Calgary Canada Bound!

TERESA RETURNED TO NEW CASTLE ARMY AIR BASE from her "celebrity tour" in California mid-March 1943 to find that Betty Gillies, true to fashion, had things running smoothly. Betty had proven to be even more adept at the job of squadron commander than was Nancy Love.

That Gillies was several years older and the mother of two children probably had something to do with that. Gillies was a good listener—a trait Nancy wasn't well known for—though, according to the women who flew for her, Betty was almost as stingy about handing out compliments as Nancy was.

"Helen Mary was the one you went to if you had a problem," Teresa claimed. Betty had named Helen Mary Clark, a thirty-four-year-old mother of two sons, to be her second in command. "She was more compassionate than Betty. But only to a point. Helen Mary's attitude was 'take care of it and get back to flying.'"

Gillies's squadron, in April 1943, consisted of Helen Mary Clark, Esther Nelson, Teresa, Nancy Batson, Sis Bernheim, Dorothy Fulton, Helen McGilvery, Gertrude Meserve, and herself. Esther Manning Rathsfelder, grounded because she was pregnant, was now Gillies's administrative assistant. Before long, Esther

Seven WAFS welcome spring as they head west to Calgary, Canada, flying PT-26s (shown in the background): Pictured with a representative of Fairchild Aviation are (from left) Helen McGilvery, Teresa James, Dorothy Fulton, Sis Bernheim, Gertrude Meserve, Betty Gillies and Nancy Batson. *Courtesy: International Women's Air & Space Museum, Cleveland*

would take leave of absence and give birth to a healthy baby boy, with plans to rejoin the squadron in the fall.

Colonel Tunner had seven PT-26s that needed to be delivered to the Canadian RAF near Calgary, Alberta, Canada, before Easter. Colonel Baker chose his women's squadron commander, Betty Gillies, to make this important mission happen.

Gillies divided the group into two squadrons, took command of one, and appointed Teresa to lead the second squadron. Flying with Teresa would be Dorothy Fulton and Gertrude Meserve. Flying with Betty were Nancy Batson, Helen McGilvery, and Sis

Bernheim. PT-26s were PT-19s with enclosed cockpit hatches, with a cruising speed 100 miles per hour.

Very early Palm Sunday morning—April 18—they were in Hagerstown checking out their aircraft when Batson let out a Rebel yell as she climbed into the cockpit of her PT-26. "Eeeeyow! Hey Teresa, we're goin' back to Montana and on to Calgary, Canada!" Both, of course, had been part of that now legendary December trip to Great Falls.

The others laughed. They were used to Nancy's enthusiastic outbursts.

They took off from Hagerstown early, headed west across Ohio, Indiana, and Illinois, and ran out of daylight in Joliet, Illinois—but not before they had flown an astounding 697 miles. And the weather was improving over what they were used to in Wilmington. Winter lasted forever in Delaware! Spring definitely was on the way. Besides, these airplanes had canopies, so the pilots didn't have to contend with wind in their faces and icicles forming on their runny noses.

The next day's destination was North Platte, Nebraska, a 600-mile flight. They crossed the Mississippi River, and soon they were looking down on the cornfields of Iowa and later on the wheat fields of Nebraska. They crossed the Missouri River below Omaha, Nebraska, and cruised on into North Platte. They had fun watching the ground rise up to meet them as they flew west.

Next stop, Great Falls, Montana, 100 miles from the Canadian border and the home of the familiar—to Teresa and Nancy—7th Ferrying Group. It housed the ferrying base from which planes were processed for lend-lease to Russia. From Great Falls, male pilots ferried these planes—mostly P-39 single-engine pursuits—to Alaska. There, Russian pilots picked them up and flew them over the Bering Strait and on to the Soviet Union to be used against German troops fighting Russia on **its** Western Front. The WAFS' seven airplanes, however, were bound for a Canadian RAF pilot training facility in Alberta.

The last leg was a short one—only 275 miles from Great Falls to a town named DeWinton in Alberta. Now they flew along the majestic snow-capped Canadian Rockies, a new and awe-inspiring sight to all seven of them.

They managed to deliver their planes from Hagerstown to DeWinton in a record four days—and four days before the Easter deadline. The seven WAFS were flown from Great Falls to Salt Lake City, where they boarded an eastbound airliner and flew home.

✈ ✈ ✈

Betty Gillies had qualified to ferry P-47 Thunderbolts. Now Helen Mary Clark was the second to check out on the P-47. She did so on May 3, 1943. By late May, both Betty and Helen Mary were regulars at the Republic Airplane factory, Farmingdale, Long Island. From there, they ferried Thunderbolts to Newark, New Jersey, for shipment to England.

Teresa was next in line.

Late in June, just back from a PT-19 trip, she dropped by Gillies's office. "I was dog tired after a long flight, but Betty was sitting in the office, so I stopped in to see her," Teresa recalled. "She handed me a copy of some tech orders. I was to check out in the P-47!

"She told me, 'Whenever there's a P-47 on the flight line, go sit in it and get familiar with the operating and emergency procedures.'"

Teresa was both elated and troubled!

"Most of my flying time was in smaller aircraft. For several days I warmed the cockpit seat of that '47 and studied everything I could about the 'Jug' as it is affectionately called.

"I was scared to death of flying it. This was no trainer. The cockpit had only enough room for a single pilot—me—so my first flight was a solo! I'd heard the guys discussing the flight characteristics of this 14,500 pound, 2000 horsepower, flying arsenal! I'd learned on something with about fifty."

Teresa was aware that the designer, Alexander Kartveli, had armor-plated the cockpit to protect the pilot from injury. In fact, she was happy to hear it. "In case the engine quit on takeoff, you could plow through a building and only kill the people in front of you," she quipped.

She already knew there was no forward visibility on the ground because of the huge engine. "One of the guys said the real sweat was trying to keep the plane in the middle of the runway while taking off and landing. You had to look out at a forty-five-degree angle to keep the same spacing between the wing and edge of the runway."

Teresa was apprehensive when she heard that her mother and sister, Betty, were coming down to visit on the Fourth of July weekend. She was going to have to tell them that she was scheduled to fly her first P-47 on July 5.

"Mom and Betty were there to see me being a total wreck. The morning arrived too soon. I had butterflies in my stomach as I walked to Base Operations. Then I saw the large crowd gathered at the hangar near the P-47.

"There stood Captain Bing on the wing, waiting to give me a verbal checkout on pre-flight, cockpit, and emergency procedures. Then, satisfied that I had done my homework, he wished me luck and told me to take it up and practice stalls and spins.

"His parting shot was 'After takeoff, you'll be twenty miles out past New Castle before you get the gear up.' What a confidence builder! My heart was in my mouth."

She went through the thirty-two-item checklist before and after engine start. Satisfied that all the gauges were working, she closed the hatch, waved goodbye to Captain Bing, released the brakes and slowly taxied—zigzagging back and forth on the taxi strip in order to see in front of the big aircraft until she reached the active runway.

"I sat for several minutes until a couple of aircraft taxied up behind me. I finally got up enough courage to call the tower and say I was ready for takeoff—to which the operator replied, 'Pull up into position and hold.'

"I pulled onto the runway, made sure I was lined up in the middle, and locked the tail-wheel. Then I heard the soft male voice from the tower, 'P-47 cleared for takeoff.'

"I shoved the throttle to twenty-seven hundred RPMs. The sudden power pushed me back against the seat as the plane moved down the runway, gaining speed. I was off in nothing flat. I had the flaps and gear retracted as I passed over the end of the runway. That engine was purring like a kitten as I climbed to altitude over the practice area, eight thousand feet. I flew some basic maneuvers, shallow, medium, and steep turns. The stalls unnerved me, but I was amazed at the clean recovery."

Suddenly, Teresa remembered something her early flying instructor, Pete Goff, had told her. "Always take an unfamiliar aircraft to high altitude and practice letdowns and landings at an imaginary airport in the sky," he had advised, "You can correct any mistake upstairs!"

"So I proceeded to land at Pete Goff's 'imaginary' airport in the sky, mentally contacting the tower, reporting positions throughout maneuvering up to landing. I slowed the plane to make a downwind entry into the traffic pattern—speed 170 miles per hour. I dropped the gear and, wow, what a thud! Rocked the wings back and forth to make sure the gear was down and locked.

"I continued to the make-believe base leg, dropped two inches of flaps at 150 miles per hour, prop to 2,350, continued to final approach, dropped full flaps, cowl closed. Glide at 135 miles per hour to landing."

In the process, she discovered, again, that Pete Goff's good advice worked.

"Now all I had to do was get down all in one piece!

"I started back toward the airport, called the tower when I was close, and was cleared downwind. I entered the traffic pattern just like I practiced upstairs, except this time was for real! Turning on base leg, my heart was racing while I kept my eyes focused on the landing area. Turning final, I got a 'cleared to land' from the tower.

"As I crossed the threshold of the field, I shifted my gaze to a forty-five-degree angle to the runway to keep the plane in the middle of it. I made a beautiful three-point landing. [All three wheels touched at the same time.] I really greased it!

"The tower operator congratulated me as I rolled to the end of the runway and on to Base Ops to great cheers. All these people were applauding. They were thinking, 'She didn't kill herself.'

"I did it! Thank you, Lord!"

Teresa claimed that's when she found out the mystique around flying the big "Jug" was just a lot of male stories. "The P-47 is a real pussycat, but with great claws and silky whiskers. What she's saying is, 'Pet me gently!'"

After Teresa's P-47 checkout, Betty sent her to the 5th Ferrying Group in Dallas, Texas, to get her instrument rating. She hadn't been back at Wilmington but a couple of days early in August when Betty told her the two of them were on orders to take two P-47s to Florida.

Up they went to Farmingdale, picked up their "Jugs," and took off at 6:35 in the evening. They only got as far as their base at New Castle. It was too late in the day to go any farther. But on the morning of August 6, the two departed at 11:30, refueled in Greensboro, North Carolina, and arrived in Tallahassee, Florida at 6:30 pm.

Teresa, having delivered her very first P-47, caught an airliner back to New Castle. Betty had to take her P-47 on to Fort Myers the next day.

Teresa joined Helen Mary and Betty on the list of women pilots qualified to ferry P-47s out of Farmingdale.

Then the WAFS got a jolt out of the blue!

U.S. Army Air Forces Headquarters and General Arnold named Jacqueline Cochran Director of Women Pilots. Nancy Love would continue to lead the women pilots in the Ferrying Division, Air Transport Command, but Cochran now headed the entire women's flying program. And their name had been changed to Women Airforce Service Pilots or WASP.

"We were WAFS until we woke up the morning of August 5 and learned that someone had changed our name while we slept! ALL WAFS WERE NOW WASP."

Chapter Thirteen

"Ever Flown a P-51?"

WHEN TERESA HAD SEVERAL P-47 trips under her belt, she began to wonder when she might get the chance to fly some of the other pursuits. She particularly wanted to fly the P-51. That opportunity came sooner than expected.

Betty Gillies made the following entry in her diary on September 22, 1943:

This morning I received an SOS from Operations at Farmingdale for ALL P-47 pilots—a blitz movement was scheduled to the Republic mod center in Evansville, Indiana.

The big P-47 Thunderbolts were to be outfitted for their eventual destination, whether it be Africa, Europe, or the Pacific. The mod center in Indiana was where that was done. Betty's diary continues:

Helen Mary is still in Instrument School. I gave them Teresa's name and mine.

The two WASP and every available male P-47 pilot in Wilmington headed immediately for Farmingdale.

Betty's next diary entry reads:

We got off mid-afternoon for Evansville. Had to RON at Patterson Field, Dayton, as we arrived late afternoon. A good flight. Teresa and I stayed at the Nurses Quarters and had supper at the PX. Delivered Evansville at 10 the next morning.

Teresa James and Betty Gillies deliver two P-47s and are immediately pressed into service to check out in and ferry two P-51s to Florida. *Courtesy: International Women's Air & Space Museum, Cleveland*

Teresa and Betty both expected to immediately be assigned a P-47 to take back to Newark—that same day. Instead, they were held overnight.

Betty wrote:

The Control Officer at the Mod Center asked us if we would like to take two P-47s on out to California!! Needless to say, we were delighted. He called NCAAB and told Group Operations that he was using two of their pilots—namely Gillies and James—for a priority movement to Long Beach!!

"When we left the base for Farmingdale, I thought I'd be back in Wilmington by nightfall," Teresa said. "I didn't bother to take an overnight bag. All I had was the clothes on my back. Now we were heading for California!"

Weather delayed them all along the route. Six days later they delivered their aircraft to Long Beach. They "sold" their P-47s at the Long Beach Sub Depot, then reported to Group Operations for further orders.

Jamesy and Betty were in for yet another surprise.

"Ever flown a P-51?" the operations officer behind the desk asked.

Betty said "No." I shook my head. "Me neither."

Two P-51 Mustangs needed to be taken east! Their orders were to report to Transition immediately and get on the schedule for the next day. So they did.

"Here are the tech orders," said the officer-in-charge. "Study them, go sit in the cockpit, get familiar with it. Then check yourselves out."

Teresa could hardly believe her ears. "Check ourselves OUT!"

But she and Betty soon got used to the fact that their reputations had preceded them. They were qualified pursuit pilots. They could be trusted to, literally, sit in the cockpit of the next fighter assigned to them and, if they hadn't flown it before, figure out how to operate this airplane and take it to its destination.

Thus, Betty and Teresa began their P-51 transition. They stayed overnight at the 6th Ferrying Group WAFS BOQ, visited with their WAFS/WASP friends there, and read the P-51 Mustang's tech orders.

Friday morning, October 1, Betty and Teresa officially qualified in the P-51. Each was assigned a P-51B to take to a Fighter Group in Florida—all the way back across the country. Smog had closed the field that morning so they had to wait for it to clear.

Late that afternoon, typical for Long Beach, the smog lifted. The two took off for Palm Springs, a short hop over the mountains. There they RONed with the newly formed WASP pilot unit stationed there and were delighted to have a reunion with Esther Nelson. Esther was originally with them in Wilmington and had been reassigned to Palm Springs as part of a new squadron to ferry BT-13s and qualify to ferry twin-engine C-47s.

Bidding Esther goodbye the following morning, Betty and Teresa headed east. In Texas they ran into the equivalent of a monsoon. Betty's diary reads:

Rain from the Gulf of Mexico all across Texas and Louisiana. We literally puddle jumped our way across Texas, with short hops from one base to another. We RONed in El Paso, then Midland, and finally Mobile, Alabama, before delivering to the 54th Fighter Group at Bartow, Florida.

Betty had no further orders and took an airliner back to NCAAB. Teresa wasn't so lucky. She was given a P-47 to ferry back to Oklahoma. And so began, for Teresa, an unexpected second half added to the trip she had expected to last less than one day.

"By then my shoes were caked with mud. The humidity had been so high, my socks and underwear wouldn't dry overnight, and I had to put them back on wet every morning. Worst of all, I didn't have my uniform jacket. Thinking I wouldn't need it, I hadn't brought it with me. Without the jacket, they wouldn't let me in the Officers' Club. I had to be content with sandwiches and stuff from the Operations canteens."

Teresa delivered her P-47 to Oklahoma, but still she wasn't going home. Oklahoma operations gave her an AT-6 advanced trainer to deliver to Great Falls, Montana.

"So off I go again, in the wrong direction—1,200 miles north. I couldn't believe it. When I got my orders in Great Falls, I was afraid to open them. I said, 'I gotta have a cup of coffee first.' Then I sat down and began to read. I had to take a BT-13 basic trainer to Idaho! Wrong direction again! Finally, in Idaho, they gave me an AT-9 [a twin-engine advancer trainer] to take back to New Castle!"

Twenty-four hours later, Teresa entered BOQ 14. The other women couldn't believe their eyes. She looked awful. Her uniform trousers were rumpled and knee sprung. "It looked like I had a pair of cantaloupes in the legs where the knees belonged. Those pants never really recovered even after a couple of trips to the dry cleaners."

Teresa had covered 11,000 miles in seven airplanes. Between her three cross-country deliveries with Betty Gillies (two P-47s and one P-51) plus her cross-country zigzag with four other aircraft (a P-47, AT-6, BT-13, and AT-9), she had been gone from Wilmington for four weeks and landed in seventeen states.

The AT-6, BT-13, and AT-9 all were aircraft Teresa had never flown before. With each one—as she had experienced with the P-51—she was told to check herself out. Which, accomplished pilot that she was, she did.

Good-natured Teresa successfully weathered the test of her patience and her endurance. But she was most grateful to be back to BOQ 14 and her buddies.

Back at NCAAB, another test was awaiting her.

Dink had finished his bomber training in California and was being sent to New Mexico to train other bomber pilots. And, whereas wives were not permitted when the men were in training, instructing was a different situation. Dink wanted her to come to New Mexico with him.

+ + +

The United States and its Allies, after twenty-one months of being on the defensive, found the war had taken an upturn for them. In the fall of 1943, this resulted in a new mission for the Ferrying Division. Aircraft that were used as trainers were no longer needed. Aircraft production had switched to building warplanes—fighters and bombers—exclusively.

This meant all ferry pilots needed to be qualified to fly those large and complex aircraft, not trainers. The WASP would be out of a job, unless…

Tunner, recently promoted to Brigadier General, had a solution that worked for both the male and female pilots. He needed all his ferry pilots qualified to move the coming surge of newly built fighter aircraft. He set up Pursuit School.

The U.S. Army Air Forces base in Palm Springs, California, was the location selected. It replaced the WASP squadron of fourteen women who had reported at the end of September. The women were sent to another ferrying base. Pursuit School was set to open December 1, 1943. General Tunner's plan was to teach several hundred male pilots, and as many women pilots as could qualify, how to fly all four of the single-engine pursuit aircraft.

Once a WASP was qualified to fly large twin-engine planes like the C-47 or C-60 cargo/transport plane and had earned her instrument rating, she would be sent to Pursuit School. An instrument rating meant that the WASP had learned to "fly blind"—that is, fly with no visual reference to the ground.

This would take time and effort, but each WASP squadron commander in the Ferrying Division was told to urge her "girls" to work on qualifying for Pursuit School. And once there, the WASP would learn to fly four fighter aircraft models: P-39, P-40, P-47 and P-51. Ferrying fighters was soon to become the WASP of the Ferrying Division's primary job.

Betty now had a squadron of more than fifty women pilots. They were qualified on all of the single engine and many twin-engine trainers. But only three were qualified on Pursuit: Betty Gillies, Teresa James, and Helen Mary Clark.

Betty knew that many of her women were poised, ready to move up in transition. Once Pursuit School opened, Betty's best pilots would be sent there. Then every month or so, she would gain more pursuit-qualified pilots. In fact, she looked forward to fielding a squadron made up of all pursuit-qualified women housed at the Republic Aviation factory at Farmingdale, Long Island.

Teresa already was actively ferrying two of those pursuits, which meant she could fly any single-engine pursuit. And she had her instrument card. She did not need to attend Pursuit School.

Teresa went to Betty.

Betty was well aware that Teresa and Dink had spent little time together. In their own way, they were victims of this terrible war that was changing everyone's lives.

That early November afternoon in 1943 when Teresa knocked on her office door and asked for a leave of absence, Betty came through for her. The paperwork went through and Teresa left two days later for New Mexico. She would be gone four months.

WAFS Teresa James, Esther Manning, and Bernice Batten catch an airline flight back to Wilmington after making a delivery to a training field in Texas. *Courtesy the International Women's Air & Space Museum, Cleveland*

Chapter Fourteen

Teresa Returns to NCAAB, Dink Heads Overseas

ON MARCH 10, 1944, Betty Gillies wrote in her diary:
Teresa James came back tonight. She has been away since the middle of November. It sure is good to see her. We talked all evening.

Dink, who had been instructing B-17 bomber pilots in New Mexico, had volunteered for overseas duty and was scheduled to be sent to England with his squadron any day now. Teresa decided it was time to come back to New Castle Army Air Base and her squadron.

What Teresa had missed while on leave of absence was the movement forward on WASP militarization. General Arnold and Jaqueline Cochran had proposed the plan and Congressman John Costello of California drafted House Bill HR-4219 to commission women pilots in the U.S. Army Air Forces.

The WASP were still civilians, serving through the U.S. Civil Service. General Arnold and Jacqueline Cochran sought to have the WASP officially militarized by bringing them in as commissioned officers in the Army Air Forces.

On March 22, General Arnold spoke before the House Armed Services Committee. He presented his clear-cut case for WASP militarization. Director of Women Pilots Jaqueline Cochran, her assistant Ethel Sheehy, and Nancy Love, leader of the WASP ferry pilots, were present in Washington D.C. to witness the proceedings. All three were dressed in their newly issued blue WASP uniforms.

To date, Congress had given General Arnold everything he asked for to fight the air war. The committee approved the bill and sent it back to Congress to schedule for a vote. What happened after that was ever worsening news for the WASP.

The public was tired of the changes the war had thrust on them. Women weren't "supposed" to be in the workplace, in the Armed Services, flying Army aircraft.

Already, General Arnold had declared that he now had enough pilots to finish the war. He closed the flight training schools. He no longer needed flight instructors to teach young men to fly and released them from their previously draft-protected jobs. Now these men faced being drafted into the Infantry—the dreaded Walking Army, known for its potential high death tolls. They complained to Congress that the WASP were holding jobs that should be theirs.

Young men still waiting for pilot training slots also had held draft deferments. Now they, too, faced the draft pool where they likely would become foot soldiers. Many a mother wrote to her congressman to complain of her son's bad luck. World War I veterans who were members of organizations like the American Legion and Veterans of Foreign Wars objected, on principle, to women being militarized.

The press picked up on this. A smear campaign against the WASP began. Betty Gillies and her squadron, and all the other WASP stationed around the country flying their tails off, buckled down and did their jobs—just like they had been doing all along. But now they endured an anti-WASP campaign that was nasty and demoralizing. They were told not to fight back.

Betty was relieved to have Teresa back. Thanks to the success of Pursuit School, the squadron's fighter pilot strength had been growing steadily. But a versatile veteran flyer like Teresa was money in the bank.

As of late March 1944, Betty's pursuit-qualified roster numbered eleven. Betty, Helen Mary, and Teresa had been joined by seven newly qualified WASP pursuit pilots: original WAFS Gertrude Meserve, Nancy Batson, and Helen McGilvery as well as early Houston Training School graduates Jane Straughn, Ruth Grimm Trees, Emily Heister, and Virginia Alleman. An added plus, Betty now had Helen Richey on board.

Helen Richey was an aviation legend. In the 1930s she was a barnstormer, a stunt flyer, champion race pilot, and the holder of speed, altitude, and endurance records. She was the first woman pilot to fly the Air Mail, and the first woman to fly a scheduled airliner. And she was Amelia Earhart's copilot in the prestigious cross-country Bendix Air Race in 1936, the first time women were allowed to enter. They placed fifth.

Helen was among the twenty-five American women pilots Jackie Cochran, at General Arnold's suggestion, took to England in the spring of 1942 to ferry aircraft for the British Air Transport Authority (ATA). There, Helen had flown the renowned British fighter, the Spitfire, as well as many other high-powered aircraft. When Cochran left England to return to the United States in September 1942, she put Helen in charge of the American contingent of ATA women in Britain.

When her mother became seriously ill in December 1942, Helen handed in her resignation and returned to America. Once her mother was on the mend, Helen grew restless. She missed flying. In February 1943, she applied for the WAFS.

The problem was, as of January 26, the option to qualify for the WAFS had been closed by General Arnold. Helen's interview with Cochran should have been a mere formality. But instead of sending her to a ferrying squadron—for which she was exceptionally qualified—Cochran sent her to the flight training school. Helen became part of the fifth WASP class now training in Sweetwater, Texas. She was thrown in with women who had maybe one hundred hours, a drop in the bucket compared to her extensive flight experience.

When Helen graduated she was assigned to the 2nd Ferrying Group. Betty was absolutely delighted to have her old friend in the squadron. Like Teresa, Helen could fly anything.

✢ ✢ ✢

Teresa had been back several weeks when she got word from Dink that, finally, his B-17 squadron was headed for England. Dink, who had been issued a forty-eight-hour pass before they took off, immediately headed for Wilmington where Teresa was on duty at New Castle.

She was on orders and wasn't supposed to leave the base. But a sympathetic Betty Gillies risked court martial to give Teresa permission to leave base to see her husband. Otherwise the two would not have seen each other before he left for England. They had their brief reunion. His squadron departed the following day.

Dink and his fellow B-17 pilots and crews had their work cut out for them. The top secret but well-planned Allied invasion of the beaches at Normandy, France, was imminent.

✢ ✢ ✢

D-Day, June 6, 1943:

The eight women pilots on duty at Farmingdale, like the rest of the world, celebrated the news of the Allied troops' invasion of Normandy, France. Those eight, Teresa among them, each logged three P-47 deliveries to Newark that day and five each on June 7.

June 8 was a very big day for Betty Gillies and her squadron. As of that date, all ferrying of P-47 aircraft from Republic Aviation in Farmingdale was officially turned over to Betty and her women pilots. Betty's dream had come true!

Mid-June, she welcomed six more pursuit-qualified pilots in the squadron: Rita Moynahan, Esther Poole, Dorothy Colburn, Mary C. Wilson, Ruth Anderson, and Tex Clair. The end of June, Mary Rosso, Josephine Pitz, and Celia Hunter joined the squadron. Betty now had twenty pursuit-qualified WASP.

The rotating schedule called for eight women to serve two weeks TDY (temporary duty) at Farmingdale, then return to New Castle Army Air Base to be replaced by eight others. Betty's squadron was fully operational.

And Original WAFS Sis Bernheim, already at Pursuit School, would graduate July 15 and return to join the Farmingdale-to-Newark-bound P-47 crew.

+ + +

Two weeks after D-Day, the Allies secured their foothold in France—a major advancement in the war against Nazi Germany.

Also two weeks after D-Day, the House Committee on Military Affairs sent the WASP bill to the House of Representatives for debate. Congressman Costello, the sponsor of the bill and spokesman for the War Department, gave the following very simple explanation of the bill.

> The sole purpose of this bill is simply this, to take these women who are now with the Army Air Forces in a civilian capacity and convert them into a military capacity. That is the sole purpose of the WASP bill, and nothing else.

But the bill was doomed from the start. Representative Joseph O'Hara of Minnesota called it "social legislation to glamorize the war." The bill died on the House floor, June 21, 1943.

Veteran pilot Helen Richey joined Betty Gillies' WASP squadron, 2nd Ferrying Group, in fall 1943 and ferried many different aircraft between then and December 20, 1944, including several P-47 Thunderbolts. *Courtesy WASP Archive, Texas Woman's University, Denton*

Chapter Fifteen

Bad News

THE SUMMER SUN, not long past the solstice, sat like a ghost disk behind the murky haze that often obscured the skies in the vicinity of New York City. It would be a hot day and the humidity was up, but it promised to be even stickier inland at Newark Airport next to the docks where a massive Liberty cargo ship sat, awaiting its cargo of P-47s.

Three WASP sat at the round wooden game table in the middle of the Alert Room, cinder block on three sides and wood paneling at the far end behind the pot-bellied heater that kept them warm in wintertime. The women pilots on duty didn't need heat today. They had enough—both literally, what with the summer weather, and figuratively.

The WASP militarization bill had been defeated in Congress three weeks earlier, and they were left wondering what was coming next. In the meantime, they continued to do what they had been hired to do twenty-one months earlier—ferry airplanes for Uncle Sam.

Gertrude Meserve Tubbs was writing a letter to her husband, Charlie, stationed in nearby New Jersey. They had met at New Castle Army Air Base and had been married all of three months. Gertrude, like the rest of the WASP in the Alert Room that day, was on a two-week, duty assignment at the Republic Aviation factory at Farmingdale on Long Island.

Helen Richey sat across from Gertrude, reading a newspaper. Between them sat Teresa James, writing in her daily journal. She was catching up, logging yesterday's events. Nancy Batson was snoozing on one of the couches along the wall, and the rest of the on-duty WASP were scattered around the room reading, talking, and smoking.

They were waiting to fly. The P-47s they were to take to Newark that day were undergoing final inspections and tests prior to being released for the women to fly them to the docks for shipment abroad. Across the ocean in England, a fighter pilot awaited each and every P-47 the women could deliver to the docks.

The door behind Gertrude opened and Teresa looked up, anticipating the call that the planes were ready and the WASP must get a move on, slip on their parachutes, and head for the flight line.

The man who entered the room was in uniform, but he was not the all-too-familiar Operations Officer. He looked around the room, his eyebrows furrowing as he squinted at each of the women there, as if searching. Teresa had a sudden lurch in the pit of her stomach. In the man's hand was an envelope—the size, shape, and yellow color of a Western Union telegram.

"Excuse me, I'm looking for Mrs. George Martin," the man said.

It was like the voice of doom. "Oh my God," said Teresa.

Every eye in the room was on her. Moments later Teresa felt Helen's hand on her shoulder.

"This is Mrs. Martin," Helen said in a low voice. "What has happened?"

The man came forward, his hand outstretched, holding the telegram where Teresa could see it. "I'm very sorry, ma'am, but this is," he hesitated, "for … for you? For Mrs. George Martin. From the War Department."

Teresa, her mind whirling now, realized the man was staring at her nametag. It read T. James.

She had joined the WAFS as Teresa James, even though she and Dink were already married. She had never bothered to change it. She was used to being Teresa James. She had lived with that name for thirty years now and only a few of her fellow WASP pilots were aware she was married.

"Yes." She finally managed to get her tongue around words again. "I'm Mrs. George Martin." She held out her hand to take the telegram.

"Do you want me to read it to you," Helen asked, her hand never leaving Teresa's shoulder and now gripping it very hard.

"N-no." Teresa caught herself before the stammering got any worse. "I'm OK, I can do it." And she took the offensive yellow envelope, opened it, and pulled the message from inside.

"We regret to inform you that Lt. George L. Martin 0-753906, 337th Bomb Squadron, 96th Bomb Group, is MISSING IN ACTION."

Teresa handed the paper to Helen and slumped in her chair.

After the officer left, the women all clustered around Teresa. Helen asked her what she wanted to do.

"Go home—to Pittsburgh," a tearful Teresa finally managed to say.

Helen told the others to stay with her while she went and phoned Betty Gillies in Wilmington to get permission. She was back in no time. Helen helped Teresa out of her chair and moved her toward the door.

"I'm going to take Teresa back to pack and help her get transportation to Pittsburgh," Helen told the other WASP. "I'll be back as soon as I can."

The others watched their two friends exit, the taller one leaning slightly on the smaller one for moral if not physical support.

Teresa went home to Pittsburgh. Two days later, she received a call from Betty Gillies. "We need you, Teresa. You know we're desperate for every pilot we can get."

Teresa was never one to hide and lick her wounds, and by then she'd had her fill of family sympathy. Besides, she was itching to get her hands back on the stick and throttle of a P-47.

"I'm better off flying and being with the girls," Teresa told Betty. "I'll be back tomorrow."

She returned to the BOQ in Wilmington the following day. Betty immediately sent her back to Farmingdale to move the P-47s.

Teresa's time at the Republic factory in Farmingdale was split between ferrying P-47 "Jugs" and flying the chase plane, the C-60. Some days she flew a Jug to Newark and, on the way back, served as copilot with either Nancy Batson or Gertrude Tubbs, whichever one was hauling the rest of the P-47 pilots back to Farmingdale. Early on Betty had sent Teresa, Nancy, and Gertrude to transition to learn to fly the twin-engine C-60. Thus the women P-47 pilots could be brought back to Farmingdale immediately, ready to fly yet another P-47 to Newark.

Dink had been stationed in Snetterton Heath, England, assigned to the 337th Bombardment Squadron, 96th Bombardment Group. On June 22, sixteen days after D-Day, Dink's squadron took off on a raid over northern France. His plane was hit and had not returned to base, but nothing else was known. He was classified as missing on an operational mission.

In mid July, Teresa received Dink's last letter—written on June 21, postmarked June 22, the day his plane was shot down.

Dear Butch,

How are you getting along, honey? Are you still working hard and doing a lot of flying?

We're really keeping busy over here and I'm not fooling. I'm tuckered out. If these jerks would quit shooting at us, it wouldn't be bad. I think they're mad at us though.

I had a close one on takeoff yesterday morn. I was loaded to gross and we had a 400-foot ceiling. It was still dark yet and the place was really closed in. I just got into the murk and good and solid in a climbing turn on the gauges when the horizon went out. I rolled right out of the turn and went on needle, ball and airspeed and stayed on them till I broke out on top. Whew! what a sweat. Bill, my co-driver turned about 40 colors when it went out, some fun. This place is just like a place I was instructing at.

How are you getting along with the gauges, honey? Are you driving on them yet or not? Learn all you can about them, honey, they're the best insurance in the world, next to a flak suit.

[The gauges are the instruments that make it possible to fly when you cannot see the horizon because of heavy clouds.]

I still haven't received any mail at all, it has been 2 months since I've had any. It's plenty lonesome—not getting any mail when we get home. I'd sure appreciate a letter about now. I don't know what's holding it up. I feel like a stinker, all I do is eat, sleep and fly. I haven't even had time to take a bath for a couple of days.

Enough griping now. I'm tired now. Still love me as much as ever, honey? I love you more than anything in the world honey and I always will. I miss you more every day and can't wait till this mess is over and I can get to see you again.

I'm going to grab some rest now, write soon.

Forever, "Pop"

Teresa was one of the most productive of Betty Gillies's ferry pilots. In her effort to get over the loss of her beloved Dink, she threw herself into moving P-47s to Newark or to the modification plant in Evansville, or flying any other aircraft Betty needed delivered. In spite of that, the WASP who knew her well—Nancy Batson and the three Helens, McGilvery, Richey, and Clark—described Teresa as a shadow of her former fun-loving self.

But Teresa had remarkable come-back powers, as witnessed in her early flying days when she admitted to being terrified. Slowly, she returned to her effervescent self.

Teresa and Ten Grand are Newark Bound. *Courtesy: WASP Archive, Texas Woman's University Library, Denton*

Chapter Sixteen

Ten Grand

THE LATTER PART OF JULY 1944 brought the WASP ferry pilots what could have been devastating news—but turned out not to be. General William H. Tunner, the man who listened to Nancy Love two years earlier, believed in the possible, and was responsible for the first twenty-eight WAFS becoming Army ferry pilots, had been reassigned.

He was to take command of the Air Transport Command's vital Hump Operation in the China-Burma-India Theater of War on the other side of the world. His leaving, as of August 1, 1944, loomed as a potentially serious blow to the WASP of the Ferry Command. As it turned out, General Tunner's replacement, General Robert E. Nowland, was totally supportive of his women flyers. They had lucked out.

Then news of a different sort caught up with them.

After the cancellation of additional WASP training at Sweetwater, Texas, back in June, Jackie Cochran had drafted a report on the WASP for General Arnold. It was aimed at achieving the withheld militarization. She had not given up hope.

The report was to be released to the press on August 8, 1944. But influential newspaper columnist Drew Pearson broke the release date and published this caustic piece—"There is Still Some Sting Left in the WASPs"—two days early on August 6. Here is an excerpt:

Arnold's efforts to side-track the law by continuing to use the WASP while more than 5000 trained men pilots, each with an average of 1250 flying hours, remain idle and hundreds of Air Corps pilots retiring from combat are anxious to stay in the Army as transport ferry pilots. ... Magnetic Miss Cochran seems to have quite a drag with the "brass hats."

Unfortunately, this negative and critical article gave additional ammunition to WASP detractors like the veterans groups and the easily swayed, uninformed public. Few people truly understood how much the by then nearly one thousand women known as WASP were doing for the war effort.

The WASP ferry pilots established a new record when they completed 953 aircraft deliveries within the United States in June 1944. Of those, 529 were pursuit deliveries—critically needed fighters. This was quite a feat and should have been celebrated for the accomplishment it was. These competent women pilots were ferrying large, complex aircraft from the manufacturing facilities to air bases around the nation, without delay. This meant male pilots abroad would have these aircraft to fly in combat.

But in the current climate of public opinion, this fact was overlooked.

On August 15, 1944, the Ferrying Division released 126 women pilots who were not qualified to fly pursuit-class aircraft. They were sent back to the Flying Training Command for reassignment to flying jobs that did not require flying pursuit aircraft.

Betty Gillies had to release thirty of her "girls," many of whom liked serving under her and didn't want to leave. They grumbled, but orders were orders, and the WASP squadron attached to the 2nd Ferrying Group was cut nearly in half.

Fortunately, the WASP corps of much-needed pursuit pilots did continue to grow. By August 1, 1944, the WASP had ninety

Jackie Cochran (second from left), Helen Dettweiler (her WASP assistant), and NCAAB pursuit ferry pilots Marianne Beard, Helen Richey, Gwen Cowart, Liz Pearce, Teresa James, Jo Pitz (behind Teresa), Gertrude Meserve Tubbs, and Betty Gillies attended the ceremony at the Republic factory for the unveiling of Ten Grand!
Courtesy: International Women's Air & Space Museum, Cleveland

pursuit-qualified pilots actively ferrying these aircraft. Forty more WASP entered Pursuit School between mid-July and October 1, of whom thirty-one graduated. The last two women did so on October 15, 1944. No women were sent to Pursuit School after that.

In mid-September 1944, Republic Aviation put out word that it was nearing production of its $10,000^{th}$ P-47 Thunderbolt.

The first P-47 destined for combat had rolled off the line on March 18, 1943. Five thousand employees made up the Republic workforce at that point. Now, eighteen months later, 24,450 individuals—more than half of them women—were working at the Farmingdale plant. Production efficiency had improved as Republic worked hard to meet the Army's increased "road to victory" demands.

Production cost of the 10,000th P-47 Thunderbolt—known as "Ten Grand"—that came off the line September 20, 1944, was $45,000 (in 1944 dollars). The original cost per P-47 in 1943 was $68,750.

Republic Aviation Farmingdale Division had just earned the War Department's coveted Army/Navy Production Award for the third time.

And who delivered "Ten Grand" to Newark?

Teresa James, of course.

Teresa described her unique relationship with "Ten Grand."

On September 21, 1944, they rolled Ten Grand through a paper curtain and out of the hangar door for delivery to the Army.

Everybody was there. Betty Gillies, Gertrude Meserve, Helen Richey, all the other Farmingdale WASP, and Lt. Joe Tracy who checked most of us WAFS out at Wilmington back in '42. And, of course, Jackie Cochran was there along with The Brass—President of Republic Aviation, Mr. Alfred Marchev, the Under Secretary of War Robert P. Patterson, and a bunch of other uniforms … and the entire Thunderbolt workforce. They were a big part of the festivities.

I remember the Mitchel Field band led a march around the buildings and everybody applauded like crazy. There were a bunch of speeches, then they started to pull the aircraft up to the stand and the rope broke. They ended up having to push Ten Grand up to where Jackie stood, holding a bottle of champagne.

She was up on a lift-truck platform and she smashed the champagne bottle over the propeller hub. Then they moved the plane back and beckoned me to come on. How did I get chosen to fly Ten Grand? This was crazy.

Betty Gillies came up with the idea. She had a book of matches. She said, "Whoever comes up with the shortest." She held them up and let each of us pick out the match we wanted. I wound up with the short one.

That's how I happened to take Ten Grand on its flight to Newark.

The tow-rope broke, so Republic employees had to push Ten Grand through the paper banner into full view of the crowd gathered in Farmingdale for the big event. *Author's personal collection*

When they beckoned to me to come forward, I did, and I posed for a bunch of pictures. Got tired of that pretty fast. Then I climbed up and they took a whole lot more pictures of me waving from the cockpit.

But because of bad weather, Teresa didn't actually fly Ten Grand to Newark until September 22.

That's when I taxied that big beauty over to the duty runway. Finally, they signaled me that I was clear to take off and—off we go into the wild blue yonder! I was on my way to Newark. No cameras this time, but it was a very big day.

Before climbing out of Ten Grand's cockpit in Newark, Teresa wrote a message in the logbook where it would be seen and read, she hoped, by any pilot who flew it. In 1945, she did hear from one of the pilots who flew that special aircraft in combat.

By the end of September 1944, the WASP pursuit ferry pilots—by then numbering more than 100—were delivering three-fifths of all the pursuit aircraft built.

The final squadron of the WASP Ferry Pilots, 2nd Ferrying Group, New Castle AAB, gathers December 16, 1944. Betty Gillies, squadron leader, and Nancy Love, in command of WASP ferry pilots, are front row center. Teresa, a somewhat pensive look on her face, is in the back row on the far left. "Andy," the squadron's housemother Mrs. Anderson, is in the back row far right. *Author's personal collection, courtesy Nancy Batson Crews*

Chapter Seventeen

The Last Supper

THINGS TOOK A DECIDED DOWNTURN almost immediately after the flight of Ten Grand. On October 3, 1944, word came that the WASP would be deactivated on December 20. Letters notifying them of deactivation were delivered on October 8 to all active WASP.

Teresa didn't fly just P-47s the last three months of 1944. She, like all the other WASP ferry pilots, took her share of war-weary aircraft to "the boneyard." She delighted in telling about ferrying beat-up aircraft and about some of her harrowing experiences. The story of the shot-up A-25 flight that opened this book was just one of them.

In October, when Teresa still hadn't heard anything more about Dink, Helen Richey wrote to her friend General Jimmy Doolittle, now based in England. She asked him to check on Dink's disappearance for Teresa.

Doolittle had become famous for leading the flight of sixteen twin-engine B-25 bombers in a surprise bombing raid on Tokyo, on April 18, 1942. In an unprecedented move—a true first—the bombers launched from an aircraft carrier, the *USS Hornet*. Each plane carried a crew of five. The plan called for them to bomb military targets in Japan and to continue westward to land in China.

That April 1942 flight was America's answer to and retaliation for Japan's surprise bombing of Pearl Harbor on December 7, 1941.

General Doolittle looked into Dink's disappearance. He learned that on June 22, 1944, sixteen days after D-Day, Dink's squadron took off on a raid over northern France. His plane was hit and had not returned to base, but nothing else was known. He was classified as missing on an operational mission.

From that time on, Teresa chose to assume that Dink was a prisoner of war in Germany and that he would come home when the war was over.

On October 17, Betty Gillies noted in her diary:

Currently at Farmingdale—Batson and James are handling the C-60 flights. On the P-47s are Esther Poole, Ruth Adams, Liz Pearce, Nancy Baker, Emily Hiester and me. Good weather. Each of the gals got in two deliveries both days. Ships smooth as silk!

The women pilots of the Ferrying Division continued to fly as December 20, their own D-Day—"Deactivation Day"—approached. They were still needed. Pursuit aircraft were coming off the assembly lines faster than the ferry pilots could deliver them. And every airplane was vitally needed overseas to win an extremely intense war, on the ground and in the air. In Europe, the crucial Battle of the Bulge was about to begin in Belgium.

The evening of December 17, 1944, the seven Original WAFS still flying for the 2nd Ferrying Group, along with the rest of their WASP Squadron, gathered at the New Castle Army Air Base Officers' Club. The women dubbed it "The Last Supper." Nancy Love flew in from Ferrying Division Headquarters in Cincinnati, Ohio, for the occasion. Thirty-eight were in attendance.

Dressed not in their original WAFS uniforms, but in their recently issued blue WASP uniform jackets and skirts and their silver wings, the eight sat—Last Supper style—at the head table. Betty Gillies, squadron commander, and Nancy Love were in the center. To Nancy's right were Nancy Batson, Helen McGilvery, and Gertrude Meserve Tubbs. To Betty's left was her assistant

"The Last Supper," New Castle AAB, December 16, 1944. *Author's personal collection, courtesy Nancy Batson Crews*

squadron leader Helen Mary Clark, Teresa James, and Sis Bernheim.

The rest of the squadron, thirty graduates of Houston or Sweetwater also attired in their WASP dress uniforms, sat at tables down each side of the head table, making a "U."

The dinner was chicken a la king, sweet potato croquets, fresh fruit, chocolate eclairs, and rare French wine to help with the toasts, which were sometimes long and often teary. For each of the women, it was the end of something very, very good.

Finally, the thirty-eight weary WASP found the exhaustion of emotion to be too much. They said goodnight and went back to BOQ 14, most of them to finish packing.

The next day, Betty sent Teresa and Nancy Batson up to Farmingdale to shut down the operation at Republic Aviation.

They finished closing up on December 19, then each prepared to fly her last P-47 over to Newark.

Teresa aptly describes her final flight as:

Fifty miles as the crow flies. It was known as the "gear up-gear down" flight, a straight shot to Newark, almost due west. Thirty minutes in the air, max, unless the fog came in. Then it was circle, circle, circle. There was always smoke and haze over the New York City area.

Nancy Batson climbs into a P-47 for her trip around the Statue of Liberty. *Author's personal collection, courtesy Nancy Batson Crews*

Today, they were lucky. Not much haze. Right before they took off, Nancy told Teresa she was going to detour slightly and say goodbye to the Statue of Liberty in New York Harbor.

Nancy planned to take her eight-millimeter camera in the cockpit with her.

"I circled New York Harbor and shot some footage of Miss Liberty to show the folks at home when the war was over," she told this author years later.

Nancy taxied out to the runway, Teresa right behind her. Both stopped to await the tower's permission to take off.

"Cleared for takeoff."

Nancy's P-47M began its forward roll. Gaining momentum, the 14,720-pound, 2100-horsepower warplane sped down the runway, lifting off with an ease that belied its size and might.

Meanwhile, Teresa waited, her toes pressed hard on the brakes, holding her P-47 in place. The Jug trembled, ready to fly.

"Cleared for takeoff."

Teresa shoved the throttle to the firewall and lifted her feet from the brakes. Unleashed, the Jug surged, gathered speed, and raced down the runway. Teresa gloried in the power, the ride. The big fighter aircraft lifted from the runway and climbed out and away. She knew it was the last time she would ever feel that rush. She'd never again fly anything that powerful, that big, that awesome.

When the Statue of Liberty loomed ahead, Nancy and Teresa banked their Jugs left into climbing turns and flew counter-clockwise around Miss Liberty's crowned head. They circled the stately woman who stands in New York Harbor, holding the torch that welcomes the "huddled masses yearning to breathe free" to America.

Today, aircraft are forbidden to do that. But it was a different time.

In that instant, Teresa knew what she and her fellow women ferry pilots had done for the war effort was, in fact, a key element in what now appeared to be a victory, at least in Europe.

Their Miss Liberty circuit complete, Nancy and Teresa banked and turned their aircraft toward Newark, New Jersey. Teresa waggled her wings and took the lead. Nancy followed her in.

Teresa felt her wheels touch down on the runway. Yes! Once again—and for the last time—she had greased her customary three-point landing. She continued her rollout down the runway until the Jug slowed enough for her to take the turnoff leading to the parking apron. A "Follow Me" Jeep awaited her and led her to her assigned parking place.

She cut the switches and cleaned up the cockpit, dropped her earphones on the seat, then climbed out. In the distance she saw

Nancy turning off the runway and begin to taxi her Jug behind a Follow-Me Jeep.

Teresa proceeded to Operations to sell her airplane back to the U.S. Government. From the time she signed the ship's papers—before she climbed into the cockpit in Farmingdale and until she signed and turned in the paper at Operations Newark—she had been totally responsible for, in fact technically owned, that aircraft. It was an everyday occurrence in the life of a WASP ferry pilot.

She chatted momentarily with the Operations Officer, then turned away from the desk just as Nancy walked up behind her. They said nothing to each other, just nodded.

Teresa knew if she said a word, she'd break down, right there in public, although both she and Nancy had drilled into themselves a toughness sufficient to hold back any emotion that lurked in the shadows of their minds.

This was IT!

Teresa waited as Nancy signed off on her paperwork. Then her friend turned and walked over to where Teresa waited. Together, they walked out to catch the shuttle plane that would fly them back to Farmingdale, and from there to the NCAAB.

They had made their last delivery as WASP. Inside, they were heartbroken. Outwardly, it was just another trip, another day at the office.

Back at New Castle Army Air Base mid-afternoon, Teresa and Nancy turned in their flying gear, parachutes, the fleece-lined jackets, and their guns.

The WASP who flew pursuit were required to carry a handgun. Many pursuits carried secret installations. If it looked like the airplane might fall into enemy hands, they had their orders. They were supposed to shoot the plane—not the enemy—in order to destroy the top-secret equipment the aircraft carried. There was a little red button that, if pushed, would cause the aircraft to self-destruct.

Both Teresa and Nancy had been told—in case of impending capture—to "shoot the red button."

That evening, the two friends joined others for dinner at the Officer' Club. They said goodnight for the last time and went back to BOQ 14 to finish packing.

"When I was all finished, I was crushed," Nancy recalled.

Later that evening, a male voice outside shouted, "Fire!"

Teresa, Nancy, Betty Gillies, Helen Richey, and any others remaining in BOQ 14—clad in bathrobes and coats—headed out into the cold December night. The Officers' Club was in flames.

The women joined the crowd of male officers outside the building that had been their haven for twenty-seven months. As the building began to collapse, Nancy hollered, "Let it burn! Let it burn!"

"Yeah," said Teresa, "let it burn."

✢ ✢ ✢

Teresa's recollection of December 20, 1944—her final day as a WASP—is this:

"I remember it like it was yesterday when I walked out that gate. Something died right there. After flying for twenty-seven months with these women like you were sisters, flying around the country and then coming back and chatting about it—just like a big family, and then all of a sudden you lose that.

"How could we go home to people who didn't understand? We became part of each other because we could talk about what happened, the scary moments, and bolster each other. We became very close, and all of a sudden this association has ended. A letdown like this is bound to create a problem for a lot of people. There was a great deal of alcoholism afterwards—we had to get lost in something.

"Fortunately for me, my parents had the family flower business, so I got lost in work. I felt sorry for the girls who didn't have families to go back to.

"I was devastated when we were disbanded. I tried to get into the Chinese Air Force. They wrote me a nice letter saying they didn't need pilots. I tried the airlines and they all told me public opinion wouldn't permit a female pilot in the cockpit, even if she had a four-engine rating. So I went back to flight instruction, but there were very few students after the war. Private aviation was at a low ebb."

✈ ✈ ✈

Air Force Commissions for WASP

The U.S. Army Air Forces became the U.S. Air Force in 1948. No longer a part of the Army, the Air Force was now a separate service.

Teresa received the following letter:

In recognition of the outstanding service rendered by women pilots, the Air Force will offer United States Air Force Reserve commissions to those members of the Women Airforce Service Pilots desiring and qualifying for such status. The Air Force is pleased to offer you a commission as a major in the Reserve.

According to the Official WASP Roster, several of the original WAFS took these commissions, though they were informed that their commissions did not include flying. Nancy Love became a lieutenant colonel; Betty Gillies, Helen Mary Clark, B.J. Erickson, Sis Bernheim, Del Scharr, Lenore McElroy, and Teresa James—all majors; and Esther Nelson, captain. Bernice Batten accepted a slot in the U.S Marine Corps and rose to the rank of E-3.

Teresa remained in the Air Force Reserve for 28 years. Most of her Air Force work was done in and around her native Pittsburgh, but from 1961 to 1965, she was assigned to the 5040th Air Base Group, Elmendorf AFB, Alaskan Air Command, Anchorage. She worked on casualty assistance and received two commendations. While living in Alaska, she gained experience in bush flying on skis and floats. She retired from the U.S. Air Force in 1976.

Teresa in later years. *Courtesy: International Women's Air & Space Museum, Cleveland*

Chapter Eighteen

Dink—D-Day Plus Forty Years

BEING SENT HOME created a huge void in the women pilots' lives. Doing what one could to help win the war was on every American's mind back in those days from 1942 to 1945. Patriotism was at an all-time high.

Once an integral part of a mighty war machine, overnight the WASP were nothing—cast aside and forgotten like yesterday's garbage. They felt like they were being patted on the head and told: "You've been good little girls. Now go home, get married, and have babies." They were devastated.

For women like Nancy Batson and Teresa James, and the other WASP pursuit ferry pilots, deactivation meant stepping out of the cockpit of a hot P-47 or P-51 for the LAST time—ever—and walking away. They knew they would never again fly anything remotely as fast, as powerful, as exciting as those aircraft they nicknamed "peashooters." And they had to walk away knowing that their job wasn't finished. World War II was not yet over, nor would it be until August 1945.

For one who lived life with such *joie de vivre*, Teresa James had known her share of tragedy. Like many women of her era, she married in wartime haste, spent precious little time with her bomber-pilot husband before he was sent overseas, and then learned that he was missing in action.

Finally, she did receive a letter signed by General Ira C. Eaker, Deputy Commander, Army Air Forces. The letter was dated July 26, 1945. The U.S. Army had officially declared George "Dink" Martin dead. But for Teresa, his disappearance still was cloaked in mystery. She never was certain of Dink's death until 1984.

Here's the rest of the story Teresa calls "D-Day Plus Forty."

In 1984, the P-47 Thunderbolt pilots' reunion was to be held in Paris, France. Teresa and most of the women who flew "The Jug" were enthusiastic members of the P-47 Thunderbolt Association. Planning to attend, Teresa began to search through some of her old correspondence from the war. She found the name of the mayor of Joinville-le-Pont, where Dink's plane went down, and wrote to him. Monsieur le Maire Guy Gibout (now the former mayor), in turn, wrote to Roger Belbeoch, the President of the Veterans Association in that area, and both men asked Teresa to visit when she came to Paris for the reunion.

She also wrote to Levon Agha-Zarian, a former British Royal Air Force pilot who flew the P-47, was now the president of the P-47 Thunderbolt Association and living in France. He also corresponded with Mayor Gibout and made a discovery.

He wrote to Teresa that, "there are people in Joinville-le-Pont who saw your husband George crash. Have spoken with the authorities—they await your visit." She also heard from Roger Belbeoch who wrote: "I can already tell you that I have found people who witnessed what happened."

On Sunday, May 27, 1984—the French Mother's Day, Roger Belbeoch, his wife, and an interpreter picked Teresa up at her hotel in Paris and they all drove to Joinville-le-Pont, some forty-five minutes from Paris. They were met by the current mayor, Pierre Aubry, and a crowd of people. This is what Teresa wrote about that day:

I saw a plaque that said, "In Memory of George L. Martin." And there was a piece of B-17 landing gear in the niche. After a welcoming speech, a caravan of cars drove out Avenue de Lille to the crash site.

We pulled up in front of the house that the wing had hit. The woman who was living there during the war still lived there. She was in her 80s. Through an interpreter I talked to this dear lady who said she was in her house when the plane crashed. She described to me her feelings about the crash and how it was a miracle that the plane stayed in the middle of the narrow street.

A memorial plaque on the wrought-iron fence out front said, "In Honor of the Nine American Airmen Who Gave Their Lives for Freedom, June 22, 1944."

I was overcome with sadness. All I could think of was Dink's last letter, which bore the same date. Then we walked over to the garage where two 17-year-old boys hid when they heard the air raid siren back in 1944. They heard the crash moments later, and when they peeked out the door, they saw the smoking wreckage and a body lying between two trees. The body was intact. They rushed him to the hospital, but he was already dead. The man was my husband. The neighbors ran into the street and gathered pieces of bodies before the Germans arrived. They were later taken to Church for blessing, and then buried together.

Then Teresa was introduced to the two "boys." They were fifty-seven years old in 1984, and they still lived in Joinville-le-Pont.

Teresa asked why everything and everyone was still there forty years later. She was told, "People in France don't move, they don't change, they just stay in the same place." Even the trees were still there where the boys had picked up Dink's body. Teresa later found out that all the activity involved with Dink's crash had saved the Joinville-le-Pont bridge from being blown up, for which the townspeople remained thankful.

I just stood there and cried and cried. I felt like such a dope. But I could visualize Dink trying to get the B-17 down that narrow street between the houses, averting real tragedy as far as the townspeople were concerned.

Finally—after a seven-course dinner in a posh restaurant—emotionally drained, Teresa was delivered back to Paris.

At last, I knew what really happened to my husband. May 27, 1984, was a day to remember, an incredible event that ended forty years of uncertainty.

Six WAFS attended the 1999 Reunion held at the Southern Museum of Flight, Birmingham, Alabama: Barbara "BJ" Erickson London, Gertrude Meserve Tubbs LeValley, Nancy Batson Crews, Florene Miller Watson, Teresa James Martin, and Barbara Poole Shoemaker. *Photo by the Author*

Epilogue

A WAFS Reunion in 1999

A WAFS Reunion in 1999 ... as told by the author, who was there
THE WAFS HELD A COUPLE of informal reunions after the war—one back in Wilmington, Delaware, in the early 1950s, and another at Helen Mary Clark's house on Martha's Vineyard, Massachusetts. Now, forty years later, one more was in the works. In June 1999, when the five youngest among the then nine surviving WAFS were approaching their eightieth birthdays, Nancy Batson Crews hosted a reunion in her hometown, Birmingham, Alabama.

Nancy and I had met in 1992 and stayed in touch. She knew I was interested in learning more about the original WAFS' story. When we got together again in May 1999, I asked her if she would consider letting me write her biography. She, instead, asked me to write the story she so very much wanted told—the story of Nancy Love and the WAFS. Of course, I said yes.

Nancy Batson Crews decided then and there to hold a reunion—to give me the opportunity to meet, get to know, and interview each of these women about their WAFS service. That's why, when I arrived at Nancy's house on June 20, Teresa James was already there. She had come a little early for a long-overdue visit with her pal Batson.

Nancy's co-host for this WAFS reunion was the Southern Museum of Flight, located next to the Birmingham Municipal

Airport. Our first morning, we gathered for a tour of the museum. That afternoon, the museum hosted a WAFS press conference.

Six of the nine living WAFS attended the reunion. They are pictured above: Barbara "BJ" Erickson London, Barbara Poole Shoemaker, Teresa James Martin, Florene Miller Watson, Gertrude Meserve Tubbs LeValley, and Nancy herself. Unable to attend though still living were: Phyllis Burchfield Fulton, Barbara Donahue Ross, and Bernice Batten.

The WAFS sat behind a long table. The museum director, Dr. J. Dudley Pewitt—Colonel USAF (Retired), Distinguished Service Professor Emeritus, University of Alabama—introduced them. The six women regaled the press and guests with their flying-in-WWII-stories, and they answered questions from the eager audience.

Lunch at the famed Irondale Café was on Wednesday's schedule. Fannie Flagg, Alabama author/humorist, immortalized the café in her book *Fried Green Tomatoes at the Whistle Stop Café*. Fannie's great aunt Bess Fortenberry owned the Irondale Café from 1932 to 1972. When Flagg wrote her famous novel, her aunt and the café became famous.

During lunch, Fannie called the current owners to chat. She learned that the WAFS were guests that day. She wished the ladies well on the occasion of their reunion and promptly treated them to lunch, Southern fried chicken and those legendary fried green tomatoes.

The reunion was an unqualified success. The Birmingham Aero Club and the entire aviation community of Birmingham turned out for the Wednesday afternoon reception at the museum. They were there to pay homage to one of their own—Nancy Batson Crews—and her sister WAFS.

Both Teresa and I stayed a couple of extra days and Nancy showed us around the area, including land she owned on which she hoped to build a small house, a hangar, AND a grass runway on

"It's right here on the front page," Florene, Teresa, and Nancy are saying as they brandish copies of the *Birmingham Post Herald*. Photo by the Author

which to land her beloved Piper J-3 Cub. Nancy had bought and restored an aircraft identical to the one in which she learned to fly in the late 1930s.

After that, Nancy and I prepared to begin work on what became my first book, *The Originals*. I also stayed in touch with Teresa.

In March 2000, Joan Hrubec—administrator of the International Women's Air & Space Museum (IWASM) for whom I worked—and I flew to Florida to do further interviews and research with Teresa. Joan's niece and her husband kindly put us up for our time there and loaned us one of their cars. We spent all our time with Teresa, talking to her for hours about the WAFS and their experiences. The three of us had a ball!

In early June 2000, Joan and I traveled to Virginia to meet and interview two of Nancy Love's daughters. To write *The Originals*, I very much needed to know more about the WAFS founder and leader, Nancy Love. Nancy Batson Crews had made this all-important connection for us.

When I got home, I learned that Nancy had been diagnosed with terminal lung cancer.

Immediately, I began preparations to make my first of what turned out to be four trips back to Alabama to work with Nancy on the book. We lost her on January 12, 2001. Though she lived to see my finished first draft of The Originals, she did not live to see the published book.

After Nancy's death, I still had the final pieces of The Originals to finish up. With Nancy gone, Teresa became my primary sounding board. I called on her when I needed explanations of numerous points. We talked often. Barbara "BJ" Erickson London also worked closely with me as I finalized The Originals.

Disc-Us Books published **The Originals: The Women's Auxiliary Ferrying Squadron of World War II**, July 4, 2001. Braughler Books published the second edition September 10, 2017, in celebration of the 75th anniversary of the September 10, 1942, creation of the Women's Auxiliary Ferrying Squadron.

Without Nancy Batson Crews, Teresa James, and Barbara "BJ" Erickson London, neither **The Originals** nor this book about Teresa, nor any of my other nine WAFS/WASP books (including biographies of both Nancy Batson Crews and "BJ" Erickson London) could have been written. Now Teresa's biography joins them!

Postscript

THIS AUTHOR ALSO HAS PRODUCED a documentary film about the WAFS.

During the 1999 reunion I interviewed and filmed the six WAFS. In 2018—almost 20 years later—I used pieces of that footage to make a 22-minute iMovie film titled *Six WAFS Up Close and Personal*.

Other contributors, including Nancy Batson Crews' son Radford, BJ Erickson London's daughter Terry Rinehart, and BJ's great-niece Brooke Stevens, offered related film clips that I added to flesh out the story. The film of me interviewing Nancy as we walk around the National Museum of the U.S. Air Force in Dayton, Ohio, in May 1999, was shot by my friend John Moraites of the Miami Valley Communications Council, Centerville, Ohio.

I show this film when I do book talks and educational presentations live as well as via Zoom—something the Covid 19 virus thrust on us in 2020 and well into 2021. This is the only film of its kind.

Appendix 1

Teresa James' Brief Biography

TERESA JAMES was born on January 27, 1914, in Pittsburgh, Pennsylvania. Her parents, Herbert and Catherine Agnes (Ryan) James owned the James Floral Shoppes in Pittsburgh and Wilkinsburg. She was the eighth woman to join The Original WAFS.

From the day of her solo flight in 1933 until she stopped flying in the late 1980s, Teresa flew a total of fifty-four types of military and civilian airplanes.

In 1950, she was commissioned a Major in the new U.S. Air Force, based on her WAFS/WASP service. She retired in 1976. Most of her Air Force work was done in and around her native Pittsburgh, but from 1961 to 1965, she was assigned to 5040th Air Base Group, Elmendorf AFB, Alaskan Air Command, Anchorage. She worked on casualty assistance and received two commendations. While living in Alaska, she gained experience in bush flying on skis and floats. Teresa has been featured on several video productions about the WASP.

Teresa initiated the fight for veteran status recognition for the WAFS and WASP in the early 1960s. "It was through my contact with Congresswoman Patsy Mink, of Hawaii."

Because of Teresa, Congresswoman Mink was the first to introduce a bill for legislation to gain recognition and Veterans Benefits for the WASP. "I spent a lot of my own money trying to get us recognized before anyone else ever got into it," Teresa points out. Years later, the WASP finally gained recognition as Veterans when President Carter signed the bill into law in 1977. Teresa, along with many of the WASP, was active in that effort as well.

On July 20, 1986, Teresa was honored with a plaque and a tree planted in her name at aviation's International Forest of Friendship in Atchison, Kansas—birthplace of Amelia Earhart. In 1993, she was inducted into the OX-5 Hall of Fame. On October 15, 2000, she was inducted into the Hall of Valor—New Women's Hall of Tribute in Pittsburgh. Plus, Teresa's WAFS uniform is on exhibit in the Smithsonian!

On July 1, 2009, Teresa—along with all the original WAFS and all the WASP—received the Congressional Gold Medal for service as a civilian during World War II. That honor was bestowed on all 1,102 WASP when President Barack Obama signed the bill granting the WASP of WWII the Congressional Gold Medal.

Teresa never remarried. Outgoing, fun-loving Teresa lived a life that brought her countless friends. I was blessed to be one of the many.

Teresa died July 27, 2008, in Lake Worth, Florida, where she had lived for many years.

Appendix 2

Some of the Aircraft Teresa James Flew during WWII

L4-B—Piper "Grasshopper"—single Continental engine, 65-hp. Maximum speed, 90 mph.

PT-17—Boeing PT-17 Stearman—single Continental engine, 220-hp: a bi-wing primary trainer flown by the United States and several Allied nations during World War II. The Stearman was built by Boeing and used by the U.S. Army Air Forces as a pilot training aircraft during WWII.

> More about the PT-17: Of rugged construction, it was a tandem, two-place, open-cockpit aircraft with fabric-covered wings and fuselage painted blue and yellow. With its notorious narrow landing gear, it was the perfect trainer to teach fledgling pilots not to ground loop (make a sharp, uncontrollable turn while taxiing, taking off, or landing). The six original WAFS who flew those six Stearman from Great Falls, Montana, to Jackson, Tennessee, were the first women ferry pilots to fly them. Many women who joined the later WASP classes flew the PT-17 in training. After the war these aircraft were sold as government surplus and used for many years as crop dusters in the southwestern United States.

PT-19—Fairchild—single Ranger engine, 175-hp. Maximum speed, 124 mph; cruising speed, 106 mph. Open-cockpit, low wing.

PT-26—Fairchild—single Ranger engine, 175-hp. Maximum speed, 128 mph; cruising speed, 106 mph. Closed-cockpit, low wing.

BT-13—Vultee "Valiant" (also known as the Vultee Vibrator): single Pratt & Whitney engine, 450-hp. Maximum speed, 155 mph; cruising speed, 130 mph.

AT-6—North American "Texan"—single 600-hp Pratt & Whitney engine. Maximum speed, 206 mph; cruising speed, 145 mph.

AT-9—Curtiss "Fledgling" (also known as the "Jeep")—twin Lycoming engines, 295-hp each. Maximum speed, 197 mph; cruising speed, 173 mph. Used to bridge the gap between single-engine trainers and twin-engine combat aircraft.

A-25—Curtiss A-25 Shrike: a single-engine, two-seat dive bomber, a modified version of the U.S. Navy's SB2C Helldiver. The U.S. Army Air Forces ordered 3,000 in February 1942, and Curtiss manufactured 900 before cancellation.

C-60—The Lockheed C-60 Lodestar is a military conversion of the Lockheed Model 18 passenger transport developed in 1940. During World War II, the U.S. Army Air Forces used the aircraft for training and to transport personnel and freight.

P-47—Republic "Thunderbolt" (also called "the Jug"); maximum weight, 17,500 pounds. One Pratt & Whitney engine, 2,430-hp. Maximum speed, 433 mph; cruising speed, 350 mph. Range 1,030 miles. Service ceiling, 42,000 feet. Wingspan, 40 feet 9 inches; length, 36 feet 2 inches. Taildragger. (Statistics from the United States Air Force Museum Aircraft brochure, page 21, 2003, and from the Internet.) P stands for Pursuit, The P-47 was used to search out and pursue other aircraft. Also designated a fighter aircraft, P-47s defended and protected other aircraft, usually bombers sent on bombing missions over Germany.

P-51—North American "Mustang" D model—single Packard-built Rolls-Royce "Merlin" engine, 1,490-hp. Maximum speed, 437 mph; cruising speed, 275 mph; range 1,000 miles; service ceiling, 41,900 feet. Taildragger. The P-51, like the P-47, was a pursuit plane and a fighter aircraft.

From Teresa's Logbooks

Teresa's logbooks, kept through her 43-year aviation career, show the following 54 entries of aircraft flown:

A-25	C-60	P-47
A-30	C-119	P-51
A-35	C-139	Piper J-3 Cub
Aeronca Chief	Cessna 150	Piper Tripacer
Aeronca C-3	Cessna 152	PQ-14
Aeronca K	Cessna 170	PT-17
Aeronca Low-wing	Cessna 180	PT-19
American Standard	Cherokee 140	PT-23
American Eagle	Culver Cadet	PT-26
AT-6	Curtiss Oriole	Spartan
AT-9	DART	Stinson Reliant
AT-10	Davis Monacoupe	Swift
BC-1	Gypsy Moth	Taylorcraft
Barling NB-3	Kinner Bird	Taylorcraft E-2 Cub
Beechcraft	Kinner Fleet	Travel Air OX-5
Bellanca	Mooney	UC-61
C-45	Musketeer	UPF-7
C-47	Navion	WACO

Teresa James flies the mail for her hometown, Wilkinsburg, Pennsylvania, as part of National Mail Week, May 15-21, 1938, celebrating the twentieth anniversary of American Air Mail delivery. *From Julia Lauria-Blum's personal collection*

Appendix 3

Teresa James' Aviation Timeline

Pre-World War II

October 12, 1934—Teresa earns Private License #31249 flying an OX-5 Travel Air bi-plane.

May 15-21, 1938—Teresa flies the U.S. Mail in celebration of the twentieth anniversary of American Air Mail delivery.

August 1939—Teresa earns her Primary Instructor's Rating, Buffalo Aeronautical in New York.

Winter 1940-41—Teresa earns her Secondary Instructor's Rating at Max Rappaport's Flying Service, Roosevelt Field on Long Island, New York. She's now qualified to teach Advanced Aerobatics and Inverted Flying to fledgling military pilots destined to fly combat.

Winter 1941—She lands an instructing job at Tomak Aviation Corporation in Pittsburgh, Pennsylvania.

World War II, 1942

September 6—Teresa receives a telegram from Nancy Love and Colonel Robert Baker asking her to come to New Castle Army Air Base (NCAAB), Wilmington, Delaware, if she is interested in qualifying for a squadron of women pilots who will be ferrying trainer aircraft for the Ferrying Division, Air Transport Command, U.S. Army Air Forces. Teresa has 2,254 hours of flying time.

September 21— Teresa reports for duty with the newly formed Women's Auxiliary Ferrying Squadron (WAFS) at NCAAB.

October 19—Teresa and seven other women graduate from their thirty-day orientation into the Ferrying Division, Air Transport Command. They are officially the first members of the Women's Auxiliary Ferrying Squadron, the WAFS.

October 23-24—Teresa is one of six WAFS assigned to the squadron's first ferrying flight. They deliver six L-4B Piper Cubs to Mitchel Field on Long Island, New York.

November 10—Second WAFS trip: she's one of seven WAFS to ferry L-4B Cubs south.

November 22—First PT-19 delivery: Teresa is one of eleven WAFS assigned.

December 4—Nancy Love appoints Teresa flight leader. She and five other WAFS board the train for a journey to Great Falls, Montana, to pick up six Stearman PT-17 aircraft and deliver them to Jackson, Tennessee.

December 31—Teresa and the others deliver their PT-17s to Jackson, Tennessee, after several weather delays.

1943

February 18—Teresa is assigned to take a PT-19 from Hagerstown, Maryland, to Hollywood, California, alone. A coast-to-coast trip. She returns to Base on March 11. The aircraft is to be used in a movie.

July 5—Teresa flies her first P-47.

October 1—Teresa flies her first P-51.

November—Teresa takes a leave of absence to spend time with Dink.

1944

March 10—Teresa returns to the squadron at NCAAB.

June 6—D-Day, the day the Allied Forces land in Normandy, France. Teresa and five other women each deliver three P-47s to Newark, New Jersey, to celebrate the invasion.

September 22—Teresa is chosen to take the 10,000th P-47—Ten Grand—built at the Republic Factory in Farmingdale, New York, and deliver it to the docks at Newark, New Jersey, to be shipped to England and used in the war in Europe.

October 3—Word arrives that the WASP are to be disbanded on December 20.

December 18-19—Teresa and Nancy Batson close up the ferrying operation at Republic Aviation in Farmingdale for squadron leader Betty Gillies and each delivers her last P-47 to Newark.

December 20—The WASP are sent home.

Teresa continues flying whenever possible after World War II.

Appendix 4

Glossary and Acronyms of WWII Aviation and Military Terms Used

AAB—Army Air Base

AAF—Army Air Forces

AT—Advanced Trainer; aircraft flown in the third of three-stage military flight instruction

ATA—Air Transport Auxiliary (women ferry pilots attached to the British Royal Air Force)

ATC—Air Transport Command (U.S. Army Air Forces)

Biplane/biwing—An airplane with two wings, one below and one above the cockpit

BOQ—Bachelor Officer Quarters

BT—Basic Trainer; aircraft flown in the second of three-stage military flight instruction

CAVU—Ceiling and Visibility Unlimited; no clouds above or below the aircraft to impair visibility

Ceiling—Vertical distance from ground to cloud cover

Commercial License—A federal certificate that allows a pilot to carry passengers for hire or to haul freight

Control Tower—Tall structure at an airfield where air traffic controllers work to stay in radio contact with pilots in the area, giving them instructions as their planes arrive or depart

Court-martial—Military trial

CPTP—Civilian Pilot Training Program (pre-World War II)

FD—Ferrying Division/Air Transport Command

FC—Ferry Command, the nickname for the Ferrying Division/Air Transport Command

Flaps—*American Heritage Dictionary:* a control surface on the trailing edge of an aircraft wing used primarily to increase lift or drag. (i.e. landing, takeoff, turning in the air, etc.)

Instrument Flight Training—Learning to fly when there is no visible horizon or when the ceiling is lower than allowable for visual flying. This is known as IFR (instrument flying rules). Flying with a clear sky and visible horizon is known as VFR (visual flight rules).

P—Pursuit; designation for pursuit or fighter aircraft, as in P-47

Private License—A federal license earned by a pilot who has demonstrated sufficient skills to be allowed to carry passengers, but not for hire

PT—Primary Trainer; aircraft used in the first stage of three-stage flight instruction of military flight training in WWII

RAF—Royal Air Force (British)

RON—Remain Over Night

Transition—Instructing a pilot on how to fly an unfamiliar aircraft

USAAC—United States Army Air Corps

USAAF—United States Army Air Forces

USAF—United States Air Force

WAC—Women's Army Corps

WAFS—Women's Auxiliary Ferrying Squadron

WASP—Women Airforce Service Pilots

WFTD—Women's Flying Training Detachment

WTS—War Training Service (followed CPT, 1941-1944)

Appendix 5

General Glossary

Barnstorming—Traveling the country, appearing in fairs and air shows; giving exhibitions of stunt flying; also taking passengers up in the airplane and thrilling or scaring them with stunt (aerobatic) flying.

Belied—Opposed, disproved

Canopy—Cover

Canteen—Informal eating place

Chamois—Soft leather

Commission—Military officer rank

Draft—Selected to serve in the United States military

Fighter Squadron—A group of fighter pilots and aircraft under a commander

Fledgling—Beginner, inexperienced

Fuselage—Central body of the airplane

Ground loop—A sharp, uncontrollable turn of an aircraft while taxiing, taking off, or landing

Hatch—Access, entrance

Instrument card/rating—Certified to fly without visual reference to the ground

Jodhpurs—Wide-hipped horseback riding pants of a heavy fabric that fits tightly at the knees and ankles

Joie de vivre (French)—Carefree enjoyment of life

Mettle—Grit, determination, spirit

Mod (modification) center—Where aircraft were modified for climate and terrain encountered overseas

Monsoon—Rainy season

Pullman car—Railroad car

Pursuit aircraft—Another name for a fighter aircraft: small powerful aircraft whose job it is to protect larger bomber and transport aircraft from the enemy

Stateroom—First-class sleeping compartment

Tandem—One behind the other

Appendix 6

Bibliography

Published sources

Churchill, Jan. *From Delaware to Everywhere: New Castle Army Air Base, New Castle County Airport.* Dover, DE: Dover Litho Printing Co., 2007. (Partial funding was provided by the Delaware Heritage Commission.)

Churchill, Jan. *On Wings to War: Teresa James, Aviator.* Manhattan, KS: Sunflower University Press, 1992.

Fahey, James C. *U.S. Army Aircraft, 1908-1946 (Heavier-Than-Air).* New York: Ships and Aircraft, 1946.

Gott, Kay. *Women in Pursuit: Flying Fighters for the Air Transport Command Ferrying Division during World War II.* McKinleyville, CA: K. Gott, 1993.

Granger, Byrd Howell. *On Final Approach: The Women Airforce Service Pilots of W.W.II.* Scottsdale, AZ: Falconer Publishing Company, 1991.

Keil, Sally Van Wagenen. *Those Wonderful Women in Their Flying Machines: The Unknown Heroines of World War II.* New York: Four Directions Press, 1990.

La Farge, Oliver. *The Eagle in the Egg.* Boston: Houghton Mifflin, 1949.

Matz, Onas P. *History of the 2nd Ferrying Group, Ferrying Division, Air Transport Command.* Seattle: Modet Enterprises, Inc., 1993. (Sponsored by the Wilmington Warrior Association.)

Rickman, Sarah Byrn. *The Originals: The Women's Auxiliary Ferrying Squadron of World War II.* Springboro, OH: Braughler Books, 2017.

Rickman, Sarah Byrn. *WASP of the Ferry Command*. Denton, Texas: University of North Texas Press, 2016.

Tunner, William H., and Booton Herndon. *Over the Hump: The Story of General William H. Tunner, the Man Who Moved Anything, Anywhere, Anytime*. New York: Duell, Sloan and Pearce, 1964.

United States Air Force Museum. Aircraft Brochure: Featuring more than 175 U.S. aircraft.

Government Historical Studies, WWII

"History of the Air Transport Command, Women Pilots in the Air Transport Command." Prepared by the Historical Branch, Intelligence and Security Division, Headquarters, Air Transport Command in accordance with ATC Regulation 20-20, AAF Regulation 20-8, and AR 345-105, as amended. Unpublished. Author, Lt. Col. Oliver La Farge, official historian for the Air Transport Command. This is the accepted history on the women ferry pilots of the ATC.

"History of the Air Transport Command: Women Pilots in the Air Transport Command." Historical data prepared by the Historical Branch, Intelligence and Security Division, Headquarters, Air Transport Command in accordance with ATC Regulation 20-20, AAF Regulation 20-8, and AR 345-105, as amended. WASP Archival Collection, Texas Woman's University Library, Denton, Texas. (This is an abstracted version of the volume listed immediately above.)

"Women Pilots in the Ferrying Division, Air Transport Command." A history written in accordance with AAF Regulation No. 20-8 and AAF Letter 40-34; unpublished. Author, Capt. Walter J. Marx, official historian for the Ferrying Division. The Nancy Harkness Love private collection. A copy is also in this author's files.

"Women Pilots AAF, 1941-1944." Army Air Forces Historical Studies: No. 55. March 1946. This document also is part of the WASP Archival Collection, Texas Woman's University Library, Denton, Texas. It also is part of the Jacqueline Cochran Collection, Dwight D. Eisenhower Presidential Library, Abilene, Kansas.

Author's personal interviews with:

Nancy Batson Crews, WAFS

Phyllis Burchfield Fulton, WAFS

Teresa James Martin, WAFS

Gertrude Meserve Tubbs LeValley, WAFS

Barbara "BJ" Erickson London, WAFS

Barbara Donahue Ross, WAFS

Barbara Poole Shoemaker, WAFS

Florene Miller Watson, WAFS

In addition, the author has conducted personal interviews with approximately sixty WASP as part of the WASP Archives Oral History project, Texas Woman's University.

Eisenhower Library, Abilene, Kansas
Jacqueline Cochran Collection

International Women's Air & Space Museum (IWASM), Cleveland, Ohio Collections
- Photos

WASP Archives, Texas Woman's University, Denton, Texas Collections:
- Photos
- Oral histories
- WASP biofiles

Note:
WAFS Nancy Batson Crews and I met several times in her Alabama home between June and December 2000. We were working on my first book, *The Originals: The Women's Auxiliary Ferrying Squadron of World War II*, which I was writing at her request and with her help. Much of this biography of Teresa James comes from the same material and personal interviews with both women.

Acknowledgments

MY HEARTFELT THANKS:

To my marketing manager Mary Walewski of Buy the Book Marketing. She connects me with the wider audience I need to reach to create interest in these stories.

To my editor Patrice Rhoades-Baum, Sojourn Enterprises, Inc., in appreciation of her sharp eyes and word sense.

To my book designer Bob Schram, Bookends Design. This is the fourth gorgeous Y/A WAFS/WASP book Bob has designed for me.

To the National Aviation Hall of Fame, Dayton, Ohio, and its executive director Amy Spowart. The NAHF awarded me its 2019 Combs Gates Award for my first two WASP books for younger readers: *BJ Erickson: WASP Pilot* (2018) and *Nancy Love: WASP Pilot* (2019). The Combs Gates Award is for projects that bring to light the accomplishments of the men and women of aviation and space—the human rather than the technical side of flight. The NAHF recognizes the need for aviation literature for our youth. The Combs Gates Award has given me the springboard from which to launch more stories of our outstanding women aviators.

To Vann Nored, a fellow pilot and believer in passing the love of aviation on to the younger generations. He works with the greater Colorado Springs, Colorado, area schools that offer STEM classes (science, technology, engineering, and math). We work together through local teachers, libraries, and organizations to get copies of my youth-focused aviation books in the hands of young readers. We gratefully accept donations to fund these giveaway copies.

About the Author

Teresa James, WAFS Pilot: Gear Up/Gear Down—a P-47 to Newark is Sarah Byrn Rickman's eleventh book about the women who flew for America in World War II. Her first, *The Originals*, was published in 2001.

In 2017, Sarah switched from writing adult-focused books to writing biographies of these wartime women pilots for the Young Adult market. Why?

"Today's young women need to hear the incredible stories of these gutsy women who broke the gender barrier in aviation. The WAFS, later known as the WASP, paved the way for today's women pilots of the U.S. Air Force, Navy, Army, Marines, and Coast Guard—and those flying commercial aircraft as well," Sarah says.

Two of Sarah's books, *BJ Erickson: WASP Pilot* and *Nancy Love: WASP Pilot*, aimed at this audience, were published by Filter Press in 2018 and 2019. For her third book, Sarah decided to go it on her own. She established Flight to Destiny Press and her book *Betty Gillies: WAFS Pilot* debuted in October 2020. Now *Teresa James: WAFS Pilot* joins the other three.

Readers age 12 to adult is Sarah's new focus. Her books are aimed primarily at today's young women as well as their sisters, moms, aunts, and grandmothers, who, like the WASP, "look to the stars." Young women—and men—who are looking at future careers in aviation and STEM (science, technology, engineering, math) hopefully will find in these books the inspiration to forge ahead.

Sarah has wanted to write books since she was five years old. But, by choice and feeling the necessity of more life experience, she became a journalist first. She began her career as a reporter/columnist at *The Detroit News* and concluded it as editor of the twice-weekly *Centerville-Bellbrook Times* in suburban Dayton, Ohio. In addition to writing books, since 2009, Sarah has served as editor of the *WASP News*, the official newsmagazine for the WASP Archives, located at the Texas Woman's University Library, Denton, Texas.

Sarah realized a lifelong dream in 2011. She earned her Sport Pilot certificate flying a 1940s-vintage tailwheel aircraft—an Aeronca Champ—similar to the Cubs and Taylorcraft the WAFS and WASP learned on, back in the day. (See her Author Photo with the Champ on page 159.) She's a proud member of the Ninety-Nines International Organization for Women Pilots and is Vice Chair of the Board of Trustees for the Ninety-Nines Museum of Women Pilots in Oklahoma City, Oklahoma.

Other Books by Sarah Byrn Rickman

- **BETTY GILLIES, WAFS PILOT:** *The Days and Flights of a World War II Squadron Leader* Flight to Destiny Press, Colorado Springs, CO, October 2020 (Y/A biography)

- **NANCY LOVE: WASP PILOT** Filter Press, Palmer Lake, CO, May 2019 (Y/A biography)

- **BJ ERICKSON: WASP PILOT** Filter Press, Palmer Lake, CO, March 2018 (Y/A biography)

- **FINDING DOROTHY SCOTT:** *Letters of a WASP Pilot* Texas Tech University Press, Lubbock, September 2016 (biography/nonfiction)

- **WASP OF THE FERRY COMMAND:** *Women Pilots, Uncommon Deeds* University of North Texas Press, Denton, March 2016 (nonfiction)

- **FLIGHT TO DESTINY, A WASP** *Novel* Greyden Press, Dayton, OH, 2014 (fiction) Second Edition released March 2017, Braughler Books, Springboro, OH

- **NANCY BATSON CREWS:** *Alabama's First Lady of Flight* University of Alabama Press, Tuscaloosa, 2009 (biography/nonfiction)

- **NANCY LOVE AND THE WASP FERRY PILOTS OF WORLD WAR II** University of North Texas Press, Denton, March 2008 (biography/nonfiction)

- **FLIGHT FROM FEAR** Disc-Us Books, Inc., Santa Fe, NM, 2002 (fiction)

- **THE ORIGINALS:** *The Women's Auxiliary Ferrying Squadron of World War II*
  Disc-Us Books, Inc., Sarasota, FL, 2001 (nonfiction)
  Second Edition released September 2017, Braughler Books, Springboro, OH

A Note from Sarah

PLEASE VISIT MY WEBSITE: www.SarahByrnRickman.com. While you're there, please click on my Blog link, found to the right of my Flight to Destiny logo at the top. There, you'll find a virtual library of my blog articles dedicated to WASP stories as well as stories of many women flyers of yesterday and today. When I travel somewhere to present my books and my film—*Six WAFS Up Close and Personal*—I write a blog about the adventure.

Also, click the Subscribe link to receive my biweekly newsletter sent to all my Blog subscribers. Or click Contact to send me a message directly. Please let me know if you like my books.

What interests you most about the WAFS/WASP?

And thank you for reading my books!

Sarah's Book Awards

2021

- *Betty Gillies WAFS Pilot: The Days and Flights of a World War II Squadron Leader*—Finalist, Colorado Authors League, Non-Fiction: Biography, Memoir.

- *Betty Gillies WAFS Pilot: The Days and Flights of a World War II Squadron Leader*—Finalist, Colorado Authors League, Young Adult Fiction/Non-Fiction

2020

- *Nancy Love: WASP Pilot* —Finalist, Colorado Authors League, Children's/ Young Adult

2019

- *BJ Erickson: WASP Pilot* and *Nancy Love: WASP Pilot*—Winners of the Combs Gates Award. This award is given annually by the National Aviation Hall of Fame for creative projects that reflect an emphasis on aviation's individual pioneers—the people who define America's aerospace horizons. Sarah's series about women pilots who flew in World War II is aimed at today's young women readers. The addition of *Betty Gillies WAFS Pilot* last year and now *Teresa James WAFS Pilot* have made this a four-part series.

- *BJ Erickson: WASP Pilot*—Finalist, Colorado Authors League, Children's/Young Adult

2018

- *BJ Erickson: WASP Pilot*—Winner, Sarton Award, Young Adult nonfiction

- *WASP of the Ferry Command: Women Pilots, Uncommon Deeds*—Winner: The Marjorie Davis Roller Nonfiction Award, National League of American Pen Women, Inc.

2017

- *Finding Dorothy Scott: Letters of a WASP Pilot*—Winner: The Sarton Women's Literary Award in Biography from Story Circle Network; and also Winner, The Colorado Independent Publishers Association (CIPA) Evvy Award in Biography. Finalist: The Colorado Book Award in Biography from the Colorado Humanities; the Indie FOREWORD Book of the Year Awards in adult nonfiction/history; and The WILLA Literary Award in scholarly nonfiction given by Women Writing the West (named for Pulitzer Prize winning novelist Willa Cather).

2016

- *Flight to Destiny*, a WASP novel—Winner of the 2016 Eudora Welty Memorial Award in Fiction from the National League of American Pen Women, Inc.

2013

- *Flight to Destiny*, a WASP novel—Grand Prize, Fiction, Greyden Press Book Competition.

2009

- *WASP of the Ferry Command: Women Pilots, Uncommon Deeds*—Combs Gates Award, Winner, given annually by the National Aviation Hall of Fame for creative projects that

Sarah and the Aeronca Champ 7-AC (N1798E) that she soloed Friday the 13th of November in 2009, and in which she did most of her flying. Photo taken at Red Stewart Airfield outside of Waynesville, Ohio, on November 15, 2010, after Sarah completed her three-leg-cross-country solo. Her route: land first at a local glider field. Takeoff from there and fly to Grimes Field in Urbana, Ohio, and then return to Red Stewart Airfield where her instructor, Emerson Stewart III, awaited her safe return. It was a warm, cloudless, lovely November day and Grimes Field had a welcoming grass runway on which she could land her taildragger Champ. *Author's personal collection*

reflect an emphasis on the individual pioneers—the people—who define America's aerospace horizons.

2003

- *Flight from Fear*—Finalist: Original Softcover category, the WILLA Literary Awards presented annually by Women Writing the West for the best books published in 2002 about Western women and set in the West (named for Pulitzer Prize winning novelist Willa Cather).

1999 & 2000

- *Flight from Fear* and *Flight to Destiny*—The manuscripts of these two WASP novels won back-to-back first places in the Paul Gillette Historical Fiction Award Competition at the Pikes Peak Writers Conference, Colorado Springs.